The Agreement and a new beginning to policing in Northern Ireland

*Conference report including
Human Rights Benchmarks for policing change*

The Agreement and a new beginning to policing in Northern Ireland

Preface

The Good Friday Agreement recognised that there is now "the opportunity for a new beginning to policing in Northern Ireland" and referred explicitly to the need for future policing arrangements to be based on human rights principles.[1]   Accordingly, the Commission on Policing for Northern Ireland (often referred to as the "Patten Commission" or the Policing Commission), established by the Agreement, will be developing a series of recommendations about future policing arrangements which, amongst other things, must seek to ensure the effective protection of human rights.

The Commission's terms of reference refer to the need to consult widely "including with non-governmental expert organisations". Accordingly, as part of the general public consultative process initiated by the Commission, a number of international[2] and local human rights organisations, which have been active on the issue of policing in Northern Ireland over many years, made individual submissions to the Commission. Not surprisingly, given that these organisations draw extensively on international human rights principles and standards, there were many common issues that arose in the course of these submissions.

At the same time, both international and local human rights groups are mindful that the success of any proposed measures for policing change will ultimately depend upon their acceptance and endorsement throughout the community they are designed to serve. Accordingly, as a contribution to the public debate, the Committee on the Administration of Justice (CAJ) decided to hold a major conference in Belfast entitled **"The Agreement: a new beginning for policing in Northern Ireland" (26-27 February 1999).**

The purpose of the conference was two-fold. On the one hand there was a desire to build on the international insights drawn on in the CAJ report entitled

---

[1] See appendix I for full extract of the Good Friday Agreement relating to policing

[2] For short bibliography of the material drawn upon see appendix 2.

Human Rights on Duty: Principles for better policing - international lessons for Northern Ireland, and invite a number of leading policing experts from around the world to contribute to the local debate.[3] On the other hand, it was felt important that the conference provide a forum in which local people from a diversity of social, cultural and political backgrounds across Northern Ireland could air their views on current policing arrangements and exchange ideas about the way forward. The conference agenda, speeches, workshop findings, and list of participants are enclosed herewith.

As the organiser of the conference, CAJ was particularly interested in assessing to what extent there was a shared vision of the way ahead. Given the great diversity in the audience attending the event - statutory groups, the police, government bodies, local politicians, voluntary groups, and community activists from both republican and loyalist backgrounds - it was hardly surprising that there were areas in which agreement proved elusive. However, there was also a very significant degree of consensus. This consensus was clearly reflected in some of the concerns raised at the conference itself, and indeed in the overlap between these issues and those already raised in written submissions by the different human rights groups. Accordingly, CAJ has drawn on the findings of the conference to develop a number of human rights benchmarks for policing. It is hoped that most if not all of these measures will figure in the final report of the Policing Commission.

The Agreement calls for the development of a *"police service (which) is professional, effective and efficient, fair and impartial, free from partisan political control; accountable, both under the law for its actions and to the community it serves; representative of the society it polices, and operates within a coherent and co-operative criminal justice system, which conforms with human rights norms"* (para 2 of the Policing and Justice chapter in the Agreement). In making recommendations which seek to measure up to the human rights benchmarks brought together in this report, the Policing Commission will go a long way to securing the promise of the Agreement.

---

[3] This report (November 1997) looks at policing practice in a number of different jurisdictions (Australia, Belgium, Canada, El Salvador, Netherlands, South Africa and Spain) and looks at the good practice of relevance to Northern Ireland around issues of representation, training, accountability, structures and the management of change. Copies of the report (or the free summary of recommendations) are available from CAJ (see publication list at the end).

CONTENTS

Chapter One

Conference proceedings:
The Agreement and a new beginning to policing in Northern Ireland

Chapter Two

Appendices:

CHAPTER ONE

Conference Proceedings

The Agreement and a new beginning to policing in Northern Ireland

The Agreement and a New Beginning to Policing for Northern Ireland

Outline of conference agenda
(for speeches -see following pages)

Day One

Welcome to participants and an outline of the purpose and structure of the two-day event and opening remarks by **Dr. Maurice Hayes** on behalf of the Policing Commission.

Plenary presentation by **Ralph Crawshaw** on Police Composition and Training.

Morning Workshops on **Composition and Training -** Much consensus has developed around the need in any "new beginning" to have both a police service which is more representative of the communities served, and a police training programme which emphasises community awareness, human rights, and the skills necessary for effective community policing. So how can this be achieved and what does international experience offer?

Plenary presentation on Police Accountability by **Lee Jasper** and **Heather Ward.**

Afternoon Workshops on **Accountability at the local and policy levels including community policing -** Many people at the public meetings organised by the Commission into Policing emphasised the importance of community policing and police/community liaison on police policy and practices.   But what do we mean by "community policing" and what role should the community play in setting policing policy, monitoring police policy and practices. But what do we mean by "community policing" and what role should the community play in setting policing policy, monitoring police work and determining police budgets? How might one define "operational independence" so that the police are free from partisan political control and yet subject to effective oversight?

Day Two

Panel Discussion entitled Structural Models for Policing - **Francesc Guillen,** and **Professor Phil Scraton**. Respondent: **Dr. Linda Moore.**

Plenary Presentation by South African **Assistant Police Commissioner Zelda Holtzman** on the management of change. Respondent: **Mary O'Rawe.**

Concluding session: Journalists **Mary Holland** and **Bea Campbell.**

Vote of thanks was offered by **Peter Smith, QC** on behalf of the Police Commission.

Opening Remarks by Dr Maurice Hayes
on behalf of the Policing Commission

L adies and Gentlemen, on behalf of the Policing Commission, I would like to congratulate the CAJ on mounting this conference and to thank them, not only for doing so, but for all the contributions they have already made to the work of the Commission - through the book which has already been mentioned[4]; through their own submission, and through numerous exchanges which we have had with them, and indeed for their work over the years in maintaining a public interest in these acutely important issues.

The Commission was set up in the wake of the Good Friday Agreement and our terms of reference are set out in Annex A of the Agreement (see page 133). And that is the agenda we're required to fulfil, and no other, and that's the agenda that we will endeavour to fulfil. It asks us to enquire into policing in Northern Ireland and to bring forward proposals for future policing structures and arrangements, including means of encouraging widespread community support for those arrangements.

The proposals should be designed to ensure that policing arrangements, including composition, recruitment, training, cultural ethos and symbols, are such that Northern Ireland has a police service which can ensure widespread support from, and be seen to be, an integral part of the community as a whole. It asks us to ensure that:

- the police service is structured, managed and resourced so that it can be effective in serving these functions;
- that the police service is delivered in constructive and inclusive partnerships with the community at all levels with the maximum delegation of authority and responsibility;
- the legislative and constitutional framework requires the impartial discharge of policing functions and conforms with internationally accepted norms;

---

[4] This is a reference to CAJ's report entitled Human Rights on Duty - Principles for better policing - International lessons for Northern Ireland (1997).

- that the police operate within a clear framework of accountability to the law and the community they serve, so:
- they are constrained by, accountable to, and act only within the law;
- that their powers and procedures, like the law they enforce, are clearly established and publicly available;
- that there are open, accessible and independent means of investigating and adjudicating upon complaints against the police;
- that there are clearly established arrangements enabling local people and their political representatives to articulate their views and concerns about policing, and that policing priorities are publicly established;
- there are arrangements for accountability and for the effective, efficient and economic use of resources in achieving policing objectives;
- there are means to ensure independent and professional scrutiny and inspection of the police service;
- the scope for structured co-operation with the Garda Siochana and other police forces is addressed and;
- the management of public order events which can impose exceptional demands on policing resources is also addressed.

That is the agenda we have been given, and that is the agenda that we are adhering to. We have been asked to report by the summer (of 1999), and we are on track to do so.

The Commission is chaired by Chris Patten, former governor of Hong Kong, who has previous experience also as a Minister in the Northern Ireland Office. The local members - although we're not clearly representing anybody - are myself, Peter Smith, a lawyer, and Lucy Woods, the General Manager of BT. John Smith, a former policeman from Britain, Clifford Shearing a sociologist from South Africa but working in Canada, Kathy O'Toole, a former policewoman and Secretary for Security in Massachusetts, and Gerry Lynch, head of the John Jay College of Police Studies in New York, complete the Commission. It is a widely experienced body. From my experience of them, and my dealings with them, they are all extremely independent people who are determined to do what they think is right.

We have had representations from all the political parties, and from other interest groups, and we have seen most of them in public session. We've had a series of public meetings, thirty or so up to the moment, around Northern

Ireland. These were very widely attended. They were very interesting meetings in many ways - an exercise in participative democracy - because ten thousand people attended those meetings and a thousand people spoke. Many of them spoke with a great deal of passion and feeling, and directly represented both their own experiences of policing, and the hopes they had for the way they should be policed.

I thought that the meetings were interesting in that people said very strong and passionate things in the presence of other people who held, equally strongly, quite opposing views. And, by and large, people were allowed to state their views. That was something which had not been done in Northern Ireland before. At times, we almost became a surrogate "truth and justice commission", because people stood up and told the most harrowing stories of their own experiences - both as victims and as participants. I think that that had not been done before, and points to a problem for all of us in this society of how we move out of the past and how we deal with that past.

We received probably two and a half thousand communications, some of them just straightforward letters, but about seventeen or eighteen hundred that could be regarded as submissions. In addition there were submissions by various formal bodies. The public meetings produced another batch of probably a thousand pieces of paper where people again were asked to give their views if they had not been able to do that at the meetings. We are studying these, and actually at the back of the room after this, there are available copies of those forms given out at the meetings. If anybody here feels moved to respond to the questions, to give their views, we would be very glad to see them. Every one of those submissions, and every one of those views, is scrutinised by at least one member of the Commission - so they do not go into a sort of administrative black hole.

We have also been organising, as we were advised to do by the Agreement, focus groups and opinion polls of one sort and another - all attempting to find out what is it that people want in the line of policing. It is quite clear from what we have seen for the moment that what people want largely is accountability; they want transparency; they want a human rights approach to underwrite everything that has been done. They want conformity to the law. They want managerial control and accountability. And they want reference to a local community, to the extent that that is possible. I think that what we will see is a movement away, as the situation changes, from a form of policing which was geared to conflict control, to a form of policing which is geared to community service. And, of course, there are training and composition issues arising out of such a trend.

The Commission is still in "listening mode", and that is why we are here today as well. We want to hear what people have to say. We want to hear the debate. The debate on this matter is much too important to be left within closed doors. And so, we congratulate all those people who have made opportunities and occasions for us to hear and to talk to other people. As well as the structured sessions, individual members of the Commission have been invited here, there, and elsewhere, to hear groups in local communities, groups of one sort and another who have a story to tell. We will continue doing that, and I will certainly extend the invitation so that, if anybody wants to be heard in that way, they are encouraged to get in touch with us.

We are particularly interested to hear from young people, and in that connection, there was a similar conference a couple of weeks ago organised by NIACRO.[5] We have got some more public meetings to hold in places that we did not get to yet, or where people felt that they did not fully have the opportunity to express their views - and the more of these the better. Obviously, there has to be a cut-off date, but we are not anywhere near that yet, so I do want to encourage people who have a view, to feel that we are open to receiving those.

We have made some trips beyond Northern Ireland. We went to see police forces and policing in North America - the U.S. and in Canada. I, and several members of the Commission, are going next week to Strasbourg to take advice from people there on the whole question of human rights and its direct application to policing. The members of the Commission who come from different parts of the world and different disciplines, bring their own experiences with them, as well as their own contacts.

---

[5] Conference entitled "Inside Out - Young People and the Justice System in Northern Ireland what does the future hold?" organised in Belfast on the 9th February 1999 by the Northern Ireland Association for the Care and Resettlement of Offenders (NIACRO), Nucleus, the Children's Law Centre and CAJ.

But the great benefit to us of gatherings like today, is that CAJ not only assemble an audience of people in Northern Ireland, who are acutely interested in this subject who have intelligent and informed views to bring to bear on it, and who have direct experience of policing and policing methods. But they also bring in people from an international perspective. These speakers come from societies which have had policing problems or who have changed their picture of policing, or societies which have emerged from conflict in one way or another. We thank them for that. It is an enormous contribution to the debate. It is a huge contribution to the work we are doing. It is extremely helpful, and I look forward today to hearing what these visitors have to say as well as what people from Northern Ireland have to say.

Thank you very much.

Police Composition and Training

Ralph Crawshaw[6]

I have been asked to start this first plenary session with an overview - to initiate the debate on police composition and training by emphasising the importance of human rights to any debate about policing. I will do this in the context of international human rights standards, for it is partly by and through policing that governments either meet or fail to meet their obligations under international law to protect and promote the rights of individuals living within their jurisdiction.

As Mary O'Rawe and Dr. Linda Moore, point out in their book **Human Rights on Duty** - "There are many useful principles in international law that can be drawn upon in the formulation of domestic legislation governing police activities and powers" (page 101). Indeed the great overarching legal and humanitarian principles on which specific provisions of international human rights law are based; the provisions themselves, which are legally binding; and the many detailed codes and guidelines, designed to secure compliance with those provisions, and addressed specifically to police officials, provide a common basis for our discourse on human rights and policing - regardless of the jurisdictions from which we emanate.

I intend to approach my task by, firstly, considering the relationship between human rights and policing, and by pointing out why there can be no conflict between human rights and policing. I will then make some observations about what must be done to equip and to qualify people to become proficient in the craft and profession of policing. In doing so, I want to distinguish between two processes which must be undertaken - an educational process and a training process.

---

[6] Ralph Crawshaw served as a police officer in the Essex police, completing his service at the rank of Chief Superintendent. He is currently a Fellow of the Human Rights Centre at the University of Essex; and since 1990 has been extensively involved in the field of human rights and policing. He has worked in an independent capacity with the Council of Europe, the International Red Cross and the Raoul Wallenberg Institute of Human Rights and Humanitarian Law. Mr Crawshaw is the author of a number of human rights teaching manuals for police.

Human Rights and Policing

Even though human rights are protected by law, and any limitations which can be placed on rights and freedoms are set in law, police officials, who are described as law enforcement officials, break the law designed to protect human rights when enforcing other law. This is one of the paradoxes of policing, because when they act in this way police are not reducing criminality and disorder, they are adding to them. The paradox exists because a readiness to violate human rights law persists as part of a powerful police sub-culture which regards human rights, which are inalienable and inherent in every human being, as incompatible with effective policing.

It is possible and necessary to conduct a debate about the nature and extent of the tension which exists between "order" and "liberty", but very little of that debate can be carried through to the debate about "policing" and "human rights" for almost all of the tension has been removed by law. Under law, human rights and freedoms are clear; the limitations on those rights and freedoms are clear; and police powers, which mirror those limitations, are clear. Police, whose legitimacy is based on law, must comply with that law absolutely.

At a theoretical level there is no tension between human rights and policing. The fact that such a tension exists in practice is inimical not only to the protection of human rights but also to effective policing in the longer term.

A short term "victory" in dealing with a particular manifestation of criminality may be applauded by a public eager to see wrong-doing punished and to live in a secure and peaceful society. However, when such a "victory" is found to have been secured through unlawful and unethical means the applause of the public becomes a little uneasy and less enthusiastic. When unlawful and unethical police practices lead to miscarriages of justice and the punishment of innocent people, as they inevitably do, the applause ceases, public confidence and trust in the police is damaged, people are less inclined to co-operate with and assist police, and courts are reluctant to accept the testimony of police as witnesses. The "victory" has become a defeat.

Policing should not be a negative factor in the protection of human rights, and one of the great tasks of police leaders, and educators and trainers of police, is to develop and sustain a human rights culture within police organisations. Their task is to ensure that police organisations become and remain driven by an ethos of excellence; an ethos which is conducive to lawful and ethical behaviour, humanity, and to high standards of professional competence - an ethos which is hostile to the notion of "noble cause corruption".

This form of corruption sustains and justifies human rights violations by police, the breaking of law to enforce law, by reference to a higher "noble cause" recognised not by the law, but by the consciences of those who invoke it. The practice of policing based on an ethic of noble cause corruption is intolerable, and has no place in a democratic polity where the rule of law prevails. The "noble cause" espoused is no more and no less than the subversion of the criminal justice system, and the "corruption" which is practised consists of some of the most serious criminal offences. Apart from the fact that it is unlawful, it is objectionable because it is arbitrary as a process, and random in its effects.

Policing as a positive factor in the protection of human rights

The ways in which policing can protect all of the different categories of human rights are implicit in the provisions of Article 28 of the Universal Declaration of Human Rights:

> *"Everyone is entitled to a social and international order in which the rights and freedoms set forth in this Declaration can be fully realised."*

The reference in this Article to an international order is the source from which the right to development has been drawn by the international community, but it also includes the idea of a social order meaning the quality of life experienced at a national level.

Clearly human rights cannot be realised without social order, and social order, as characterised by tolerable levels of criminality and low levels of social tension or civil unrest, is dependent, in part, upon effective policing. In this sense policing, through the performance of all of its functions, can be seen as a positive factor in the protection of human rights and, specifically, all of the rights set forth in the Universal Declaration of Human Rights which enshrines civil, political, economic, social and cultural rights.

In addition to assisting in the realisation of all human rights through its contribution to the maintenance of social order generally, policing can be a positive factor in the protection of specific human rights. For example the right to life as expressed in the International Covenant on Civil and Political Rights and regional human rights treaties, such as the European Convention on Human Rights, requires the right to life to be protected by law. This means, inter alia, that states have to enact laws which create offences of murder and other types of unlawful killing, and the prevention and detection of such crimes is a police task.

The right to life is a civil right, and similar examples can be found for the protection of political rights and economic, social or cultural rights. Where there are laws prohibiting discrimination on grounds of religion or belief, or prohibiting manifestations of religious intolerance, the effective prevention and detection of breaches of those laws is directly supportive of the political rights of freedom of thought, conscience and religion, and to freedom of opinion and expression.

This account of the ways in which policing can be a positive factor in the protection of human rights is by no means exhaustive but it does indicate how effective policing is essential to that process.

Policing as a negative factor in the protection of human rights

Just as Article 28 of the Universal Declaration of Human Rights can be used as the basis for an examination of policing as a positive factor in the protection of human rights, so Article 29.2 of the Declaration can be used as the basis for an examination of policing as a negative factor in their protection. The second paragraph of Article 29 reads:

> *"In the exercise of his rights and freedoms, everyone shall be subject only to such limitations as are determined by law solely for the purposes of securing due recognition and respect for the rights and freedoms of others and of meeting the just requirements of morality, public order and the general welfare in a democratic society."*

The legal protection of human rights derives not only from the fact that the various rights find expression in legally binding texts, both international and national, but also from the fact that any limitations on them are also expressed in such texts.

The paragraph from Article 29 of the Universal Declaration of Human Rights quoted above is important and interesting for a number of reasons. Firstly, it is the general source of the specific limitation clauses to be found in Articles in the International Covenant on Civil and Political Rights - for example Articles 18, 19 and 21 protecting the rights to freedom of thought, conscience and religion; freedom of opinion and expression; and freedom of peaceful assembly respectively. Similar limitation clauses are to be found in articles of regional human rights treaties protecting the same rights.

Whilst the language of each of these limitation clauses varies slightly, they all require any limitations on the rights protected in the respective Articles to be specified by law, and to be necessary in a democratic society in the interests of public safety, for the protection of public order, health or morals, or for the protection of the rights or freedoms of others. In other words they identify similar grounds to the Universal Declaration of Human Rights for justifying restrictions on the exercise by individuals of human rights and freedoms they protect.

Secondly, the permissible reasons for limiting rights can also be seen as an expression of basic policing functions, since securing recognition and respect for rights and freedoms of others, and meeting the just requirements of morality, public order and the general welfare are all benefits of living in a democratic society which can be achieved, in part at least, through policing. When police enforce law by seeking to prevent and detect crime, they secure due recognition for the rights and freedoms of others - the right to life for example. In the same way, police meet the just requirements of morality when those requirements have been given legal force. The just requirements of public order are met directly when police maintain or restore order, and the general welfare is safeguarded when police provide emergency assistance to people in need of immediate aid.

The third and final reason for focussing particularly on this provision of the Universal Declaration of Human Rights is the most important. In stipulating the sole purposes for which rights and freedoms may be limited, the Declaration is setting limits on police powers. Police may not be given powers under the law to restrict rights and freedoms for any other purposes. In stipulating that rights and freedoms are to be subject only to such limitations as are determined by law, the Declaration is stating a fundamental rule of police behaviour. Police may not exceed their lawful powers.

The fact that the terms of this Article of the Declaration can also be seen as an expression of police functions indicates a significant link between the actual fulfilment of those functions and the ways in which they are fulfilled. It accentuates the connection between police effectiveness and police behaviour, challenging the argument that compliance with rules of good behaviour lessens police effectiveness, and exposing the seriously flawed notion of effectiveness implicit in that argument.

Protection of and respect for human rights are integral parts of policing to such an extent that the removal of any tension between policing and human rights which exists in practice, the creation of a human rights culture within police agencies, is one of the most pressing tasks presently facing police leaders and teachers and trainers of police.

Equipping and Qualifying People for the Craft and Profession of Policing

What police do and how they should do it

The specific functions of police officials vary from agency to agency and country to country. However, most police officials prevent and detect crime;

maintain and restore public order; and provide aid and assistance to individuals and communities in times of emergency. If the point about the positive relationship between human rights and policing is accepted, it can be seen that the protection of human rights is also a police function. It is important that this function should be acknowledged for a number of reasons - not the least of which is to encourage the development of a human rights culture within police agencies.

There are two aspects to how police should perform their functions - the technical and the behavioural. The technical aspect concerns their knowledge and skills - the extent to which police officials have the knowledge, and are equipped with those skills and aptitudes, necessary to perform their various tasks effectively and efficiently. The behavioural aspect concerns their knowledge and attitudes - the extent to which police officials have the knowledge, and have developed those attitudes and preconceptions, necessary to perform their various tasks lawfully and humanely.

The inter-dependence of the technical and the behavioural aspects of policing

The technical and the behavioural aspects of policing are dependent upon each other because if police are deficient in one of them, the other will be adversely affected. If police lack a technical policing skill - for example the ability to interview people suspected of crime, they are more likely to resort to unlawful or unethical means to investigate crime - perhaps to torture or otherwise mistreat suspects; and if police continue to rely on unlawful or unethical means to investigate crime, they will be unlikely to develop good, professional, technical policing skills.

This same logic is equally applicable to other technical policing skills and other police functions.

It is important for educators and trainers of police to understand the inter-dependence of the technical and the behavioural aspects of policing so that they are each given sufficient attention; and appropriate links are made between them, in instructional programmes for police.

Education and training

Programmes to equip and qualify people for the craft and profession of policing are usually referred to as training programmes - whatever the subject matter covered, and whatever the means of instruction adopted and the purposes of the programme.   However, there are two different processes involved in instructional programmes for police.   One is concerned with "intellectual, moral and social instruction" (to use a dictionary definition), and is an educational process, and the other is concerned with the teaching and acquisition of specific skills, and is a training process.

The educational process provides knowledge and develops or reinforces attitudes appropriate to policing in a democracy governed by the rule of law. In respect of human rights the curriculum might cover such matters as the reasons for the development of the international system for the protection of human rights; the nature of the obligations on states under international law to protect human rights; and the relationships between human rights, democracy and the rule of law.   The training process develops or reinforces skills appropriate to policing in a democracy governed by the rule of law, for example to communicate with people; to interview witnesses and suspects; to adopt the most appropriate tactics in specific situations - in fact the entire range of technical policing skills.

Broadly it can be said that the educational process addresses the behavioural and the theoretical aspects of policing; and the training process the technical aspects.

Human rights education

Education in human rights is of critical importance to the behavioural aspects of policing - at all stages in the careers of police officials.   This form of education could, for example, encourage and inspire newly appointed police officials to resist the various pressures and temptations from different sources (including the occupational culture of police agencies) to ignore rules of good behaviour and best practice they have been taught.   It could equip police police leaders with some of the intellectual and moral qualities they need to bring about cultural change within police agencies, and to carry out their command, management and supervisory functions so that rules of good behaviour and best practice are followed by officials for whom they are responsible. It could enable police officials in highly specialised roles to understand the necessity of applying their specialist skills lawfully and humanely to serve the ends of good policing in a democracy.

Some of the elements of a human rights educational programme for police have already been alluded to, and the international dimension to the protection of human rights has been emphasised. This should form a core element of educational programmes of all police officials. The inclusion of such a core element would enable teachers and trainers of police to indicate the supreme importance of human rights to the human condition; to emphasise the centrality of human rights to policing; and to reinforce national standards on human rights.

Concluding Remarks

Michael Ignatieff, in his book The Warrior's Honor" wrote

> *"There is a moral disconnection between [the] new war makers and the liberal interventionists who represent our moral stakes. We in the West start from a universalist ethic based on ideas of human rights; they start from particularist ethics that define the tribe, the nation, or ethnicity as the limit of legitimate moral concern. What many agencies, including the Red Cross, have discovered is that human rights have little or no purchase on this world of war. Far better to appeal to these fighters as warriors than as human beings, for warriors have codes of honor; human beings - qua human beings - have none."*

Occasionally, when delivering human rights programmes for police, I become involved in debates with people who assert that the situation of police in relation to human rights is analogous to that of the warrior in relation to the rules which seek to regulate his or her behaviour during combat. They argue that because police feel that human rights are an impediment to effective policing, appeals should be made to "professionalism" in policing in the same way that appeals are made to "warriors' codes of honour". They claim that, because there is a resistance to the notion of human rights on the part of police, it is better to avoid direct reference to human rights in police educational and training programmes, and simply to teach the rules which define their powers and the limitations on their powers.

These types of argument must be resisted, for there is no analogy between the role of a fighter, often blindly partisan as identified by Ignatieff, engaged in armed combat according to rules which govern his or her behaviour in such situations, and the status and role of a police official, dignified by the authority of the state to exercise lawful powers over his or her fellow citizens.

Whilst the notion of professional policing, encompassing both effectiveness and good behaviour, should be encouraged, police must be confronted with, and embrace, the notion of human rights explicitly and overtly.

I hope that these observations have provided some stimulus to the debate on police composition and training.   The list of proposals provided in the Background to Topic One[7], for which it is felt that there is wide support, contains elements which are essential for bringing about change in the culture of policing. In addition to considering these proposals, I would urge that some part of the Workshop discussions are devoted to the need to equip all police with the technical skills appropriate to their functions within their organisation, and to the link between the technical and the behavioural aspects of policing.

Sources
Bittner, Egon, Aspects of Police Work, Northeastern University Press, Boston, 1990.

Chan, Janet B.L, Changing Police Culture, Cambridge University Press, 1997.

Crawshaw, Devlin and Williamson, Human Rights and Policing, Kluwer Law International, The Hague, 1998.

Ignatieff, Michael, The Warrior's Honor, Vintage, London, 1999.

Mary O'Rawe and Dr. Linda Moore, Human Rights on Duty, Committee on the Administration of Justice, Belfast, 1997.

---

[7] This is a reference to the conference papers prepared for use in the workshops.

Police Accountability:
Lessons from the Stephen Lawrence case

Lee Jasper[8]

Good afternoon. My name is Lee Jasper and I am the director of the 1990 Trust. The 1990 Trust is a policy think-tank, advocacy and representation organisation based in London which works on behalf of the African, Caribbean and Asian communities in the United Kingdom on issues of race and discrimination: I am very glad to be invited here today. I would like to first of all thank and congratulate the Committee on the Administration of Justice whose work I have found invaluable in informing the perceptions and the views that we have pulled together post-the Stephen Lawrence experience. Although I come here to share with you some of those experiences in relation to Stephen Lawrence, I have on my visits to Northern Ireland always taken away much more than I brought in terms of experience. Certainly today's event is very welcome. I wish I could stay for the whole weekend but as you can imagine things are pretty hot at the moment in certain parts of the UK[9] and therefore I feel that at such a tense moment in time in the relationship between the black communities and the police, I need to be in London for the remainder of the weekend. I hope everybody has an excellent conference and I wish you all good luck and best efforts throughout the remainder of it.

The Lawrence Inquiry came about because of the brutal and savage murder of Stephen Lawrence. I shall not go into details of the murder on the basis that everybody has had ample opportunity to pick up that information on the TV or in the papers, and will know most of the details around that particular

---

[8] Lee Jasper is director of the 1990 Trust. He has been heavily involved in the work surrounding the Stephen Lawrence Inquiry. His previous experience includes being senior policy adviser to the Inner London Education Authority, and secretary to the Notting Hill Carnival. Mr Jasper sits on the board, or is the chair, of many committees and organisations, and has recently been appointed to the Home Secretary's advisory Race Relations Forum.

[9] Reference to the recent racist attacks and the concerns that brought Mr Jasper back unexpectedly to London are noted later in the speech.

case. Therefore, I am going to concentrate on the Lawrence Inquiry and the MacPherson report that emanated out of the public inquiry into the circumstances surrounding the murder of Stephen Lawrence. Of course, we urged the MacPherson inquiry to accept the definitions that we put to them on the issue of institutionalised racism. That was very important for black communities – that the police services of London, and throughout the rest of England, accept the existence of institutionalised racism. It was, of course Paul Condon's evidence to the Inquiry that he didn't believe that institutionalised racism existed in the Metropolitan Police, nor that race was a factor in the subsequent investigation into Stephen Lawrence's murder. He was contradicted by a number of other Chief Constables who said they readily accepted the existence of institutionalised racism. The Inquiry found institutionalised racism, and I am sure you have read and become acquainted with the definition given.

For us, there are some contradictions within the report but there is a lot to welcome - for instance, bringing within the ambit of the 1976 Race Relations Act the institution of police and other agencies that currently lie outside. The Commission for Racial Equality (GB) has made it clear in submissions about policing reforms (which were supported by ourselves, the Northern Ireland Council for Ethnic Minorities and other organisations throughout the UK) that there is a need to broaden and deepen the whole race relations legislation. That is what is needed to meet the challenges that are ahead in terms of race and racism. But in terms of institutionalised racism, we don't see that the recommendations actually, in totality, meet the definition of institutionalised racism that was offered in our submissions to that inquiry.

Largely, other than the 1976 Act bringing the police under its remit, the recommendations are essentially about greater levels of lay involvement in reform of the existing institution of the police. The submission from the 1990 Trust to the Inquiry was largely based on the knowledge we gleaned from the book **Human Rights on Duty**, published by CAJ. If you find institutionalised racism, then the response to that must be to assess the component parts of the institution of the police, particularly those component parts that foster or have maintained or have failed to supervise, monitor and expose racism within the organisation. Well, what do I mean? The British government has spent millions of pounds on improving race training for police officers and yet, in the UK you are eight times more likely to be stopped if you are black than if you are white. So clearly, a lot of effort, a lot of policy consultants, and a lot of race training, has failed to produce the kind of officer we are looking for. To that extent, we can say that the 'golden thread' or the 'trickle down' approach has clearly been seen to have failed. For us, it meant (and we stated this in our submission), that we should take away the element of recruitment and training that the police currently have under their control, and create a much more civilianised institution.

We believe that Her Majesty's seal - training, recruitment, administration and inspection of the Metropolitan Police – will need to be deconstructed in order to get at those component parts of the institution, that are colluding, hiding or failing to challenge racism. Over the last twenty years we have seen too much power being acceded to the police as an institution and this undermines the meaning of 'policing by consent'. What we want is a greater level of equitability and accountability between civil society and the institutions of the police - but not just in relation to recruitment and training.

Complaints currently go through a disgraceful Independent Police Authority, that has so far failed to deal effectively with complaints of racism and indeed very many other complaints. We believe that the institution needs to be reformed and, again, recreated within a civil society context.

Her Majesty's Inspectorate of Constabulary is the institution that goes out and evaluates the training course and evaluates the performance of individual policing divisions. We again think that that institution should not be staffed by ex-officers of senior ranks, but that it should be more civilian in character. It should be a way in which we, the public - those whom police officers serve – can check the quality of that training, the quality of that performance and delivery at local level, and thereby ensure additional accountability.

Of course, I am talking about accountability in London. Currently, the Police Commissioner is appointed by Royal Warrant and is responsible directly to the Home Secretary. We want a Policing Authority for London but we also want to examine other international models of policing accountability and that is why this conference is so timely. The present constitutional make-up under the Police and Criminal Evidence Act, and other legislation that constitutes the way in which Police Authorities are brought together, has to be critically analysed. Even where there are areas throughout the UK that do have Police

Authorities, there is very little involvement with vast sections of the community. This is particularly true of black communities, given the democratic electoral process and the importance of local authority representation. Mainstream political parties have consistently failed to select black candidates at local, regional and national levels. What this means is that there is virtually no black representation on committees, and we want to critically examine that process in order to put together a number of alternatives for ways Police Authorities can be reformed. It is absolutely essential to the project of 'policing by consent' that we have accountability and transparency. These are the issues that the community is looking at in order to develop an equitable partnership for going forward together.

Certainly, the application of international human rights standards has to play an essential part in developing an ethical police service whether in Britain or in Northern Ireland. A major failure of the MacPherson report is that although the European Convention of Human Rights has now been adopted, there is no reference to it other than the recommendation about information in internal investigations being disclosed under the Freedom of Information Act. There is no reference within the document, despite submissions from organisations such as Liberty and ourselves, about placing ethical human right standards at the centre of what a modern accountable and ethical police force should be.

We are facing very tough times in Britain, particularly in London. Since Monday, there have been three more brutal attacks, which we think are racially motivated. One was on a twenty one year old lifeguard in Luton who was found dead on Monday morning. By Tuesday, a young black boy in Battersea, South London, was brutally stabbed a number of times (he is actually the brother of a police officer). And, on Wednesday, a young Bengali was brutally stabbed in the East End of London. We have also witnessed the desecration of the Stephen Lawrence plaque. These are issues for us which are very immediate and causing a great deal of anger within the black communities. Right now in England, the relationship between the black communities and the police is so bad, that civil disturbance is likely, I believe, to break out at any particular incident which is seen to be an inappropriate response on the part of the police.

The police have failed to deal with racism in their own ranks. Even with the identification and the naming of the term "institutionalised racism" as existing within the Metropolitan Police, we still have the lower and junior ranks claiming that the MacPherson report was nothing but a witch-hunt. Many say they will have no part of being labelled as institutionalised racists. We have got a huge battle within the police force at the moment between so-called enlightened senior officers who are saying 'we embrace with zeal the notion of institutionalised racism and we are going to make sure it is addressed' and then the sergeants, inspectors and staff associations who are saying 'it is a witch-hunt, our senior officers have sold us out on this issue and we will have nothing of it'. The test is how, if at all, the project of developing an anti-racist, ethical and accountable police force will be determined by the internal political battle that is currently raging around the issue of equality within the framework of the police. How do we want to go forward?

Well, the black community's relationship with the police cannot go forward with an officer of the calibre of Paul Condon. We will be calling for his resignation because of his professional performance and his unwillingness to accept the definition of institutionalised racism throughout the life of the Inquiry. He has had every opportunity to make good his lapses by claiming and owning the problem at the time of the Inquiry and he steadfastly refused to do so. Now he claims to embrace it with zeal and is going to deliver the anti-racist project over the next ten months. It will not happen and it will not happen with black communities, because black communities have now lost faith in the Commissioner. His continuing presence will ensure that the partnership approach of dealing with this issue will not even get off first base. He will have to resign or individuals like myself, who are on the various race forums, both within the Met and on the Home Secretary's race relations advisory forum, will resign. The strength of the feeling is very strong right throughout the country. It is not a black issue - I have done public meetings right around the UK, and black and white right around the country have said with an almost unanimous voice 'this man has to go'.

My colleague from South Africa said something very poignant to me about their Truth and Reconciliation Commission: there can be reconciliation, but not at the expense of justice. We have already seen justice denied to the Lawrence family because of racism, and the impact it had upon the investigation. If we can't get those five boys into a dock, the least - the minimum a black community should expect – is that a senior officer takes responsibility for the racism debacle, and either resign, or face disciplinary action and be removed from the force. That is the minimum the black community expects and, if it is not forthcoming, then the whole project is in desperate jeopardy. I, for one, as a representative of that community, am left with no option but to present that view without compromise - with no option other than either getting a positive response to the claims that we put, or resign the very many positions I have on forums right throughout the government and the Metropolitan Police.

We are very keen at this moment to see the introduction of greater levels of accountability and international human rights standards. We will be working with a range of groups - both here, with CAJ and NICEM, and in Britain - to begin to flesh out a concrete agenda for a police service that will take us through the 21st century. Why is it that my children or myself, based on the colour of my skin, should be subjected to a different quality of policing? Why is it that because of prejudice, an institution in which so much power is vested should be allowed to discriminate in the way that it does? Our experience in Britain has proved categorically that the police service is institutionally racist, and we will need all the support we can muster from all sections of the community, if we are going to introduce additional levels of accountability and make sure that ethical standards are implemented.

We can talk about education and awareness of human rights principles and it is right to do so, but we must also think, as NGOs, about litigation. We must also think about taking cases, working together, getting the cases into court to promote universal human rights principles that will raise the quality watermark of human rights and justice within policing. The black community in the UK feels that we are almost in the position that black people were in America thirty years ago, with the introduction of civil rights legislation. There are so many areas of institutionalised discrimination - education, employment, housing and policing - that we must try to educate and inform, but we will almost certainly also have to litigate on human rights standards, in order to drag an institution such as the police which still reflects a policing ethos of the 19th century right up into the 21st century. Accountability and implementation of ethical human rights standards - these are the issues that will underpin any successful attempt to root out racism or indeed prejudice from the Metropolitan Police force and the police forces of the Great Britain and Northern Ireland. Thank you very much.

A Framework for Democratic Police Accountability

Heather H. Ward[10]

I come here today from New York City, but I do not offer any New York City or American model of policing for you to draw from. The effective oversight of a police service is a challenge which no society has fully met. As I see it, we all have a lot to learn from each other's efforts to reform and govern our police. There are many lessons, both good and bad, from other countries that can enrich our discussion of how to build or strengthen a police accountability system in a democratic society.

My work for the last few years has been to try to collect these lessons through conversations with police, government officials who supervise police forces, human rights advocates, policing scholars, and citizens' groups in various countries: Argentina, Chile, Brazil, Mexico, India, South Africa, Uganda, Poland, Hungary, Russia, and the United States. Despite tremendous cultural, political, and economic differences, there are surprising similarities in the ways in which people talk about the problems of managing an effective and accountable police service.

What I'm going to do now is present a comprehensive framework for police accountability. It is not a prescription or a plan, but a way of conceptualizing the various mechanisms to which police in a democracy are accountable. No one of these structures is sufficient on its own, nor is there any correct structure to begin with, or combination of structures that a society ought to have. Rather, we can think of them all as comprising a system of accountability. This system operates on three levels:

---

[10] Heather Ward is a researcher at the Vera Institute of Justice, a New York based, non-profit organisation which designs, implements and evaluates innovations in justice reform. Ms Ward is project manager for a major policing programme intended to survey methods of strengthening police accountability and improving public safety in many different countries around the world.

- Internal, or inside a police organization
- State, or governmental
- Social, or civil society, including both individual citizens and non-governmental organizations

These are the things which police must be accountable **to**. There are two sets of obligations which police must be accountable **for**. One is the performance of police duties, such as maintenance of order, crime control, violence reduction, and fear reduction. The other is police behavior: whether police follow departmental guidelines on the use of force, how they treat civilians, and whether they respect the human rights of all citizens. I'm grateful to Ralph Crawshaw, who in his presentation to the conference this morning made a similar distinction, which you may find more precise. He used the terms "technical" and "behavioral" responsibilities.

The following table, or framework, helps us understand the various mechanisms for ensuring police accountability. Each mechanism also represents an opportunity, a point of entry, for reforms that can enhance accountability. Together, these mechanisms make up an accountability system.

Although many countries or police jurisdictions may have a range of oversight structures, I don't know of any place where they are strong at all three levels. Instead, police, politicians, and citizens tend to argue over whether to adopt a particular mechanism and how much authority to give it. For example, police may assert that internal disciplinary procedures are swifter and more effective than external ones, while the public may confide only in a civilian authority that is transparent and independent from the police. The police and citizens get stuck in this argument over which mechanism to put in place and how strong to make it. What the police, citizens, and government officials who fall into this argument, all overlook is that they actually need these mechanisms at every level - internal, state, and social - in order to have a truly effective and democratic accountability system.

Police Accountability Mechanisms*

Accountability for ➤ ——————— Accountability to ↓	**Public Safety** (reducing crime, violence, disorder, and fear)	**Police Behaviour** (reducing corruption, brutality, and other misconduct)
Internal Control	training, line commanders, crime statistics reporting	training, line supervisors, rules, ethics codes, integrity units, administrative discipline
State Control	operational direction by elected and appointed political officials, budget authorities, prosecutors	ombudservices, legislative committees, criminal liability, civil liability, exclusionary rules of evidence
Social Control	neighborhood safety councils, community-based organizations, media, policing research and policy institutes	civilian complaint review, external auditors, media, human rights monitors, policing research and policy institutes

* From Christopher E. Stone and Heather H. Ward, "Democratic Policing: A Framework for Action," *Policing and Society*, forthcoming.

Here are some specific examples of mechanisms at each level of control and for each type of police responsibility.

Police Accountability Mechanisms: Examples

Accountability for ➤ _____ Accountability to ↓	**Public Safety** (reducing crime, violence, disorder, and fear)	**Police Behavior** (reducing corruption, brutality, and other misconduct)
Internal Control	San Diego Police Dept: Problem Oriented Policing Projects	New York Police Dept: Verbal Judo
State Control	South Africa: National Director of Public Prosecutions (carjacking project)	India: National Human Rights Commission
Social Control	Brazil: Viva Rio	Hungary: Helsinki Watch's police cell monitoring project

❖ **Internal/Public Safety**

The San Diego, (California) Police Department (SDPD) has embraced the problem-oriented approach first presented by Herman Goldstein (Goldstein,1990). Problem-oriented policing is a management approach, or department-wide orientation, which focuses on a particular crime or disorder problem. Rather than respond to the problem by making arrests time and time again, often of the same individuals, police study the crime problem carefully, analyze it, design an original response to the fundamental cause of the problem, and then assess the impact of their response. In San Diego, officers are rewarded for initiating their own "problem-oriented policing" projects. One reason for the success of problem-oriented policing in San Diego is that the message to solve problems, to police intelligently, starts with the chief and is reinforced at every level of command.

❖ **Internal/Behavior**

Verbal judo is a one- or two-day training course now taught in the New York, Chicago, San Diego, and several other U.S. police departments. The course teaches officers to decelerate conflict with words - to engage in verbal, not physical combat. With sharper verbal skills, officers should be able to coerce or control suspects without resorting to force. The course has been popular with NYPD officers, some of whom believe it has really helped them learn how to de-escalate tense situations. (Davis and Mateu-Gelabert, 1999).

❖ **State/Public Safety**

South Africa's new National Director of Public Prosecutions is now teaming up with police and community groups in Johannesburg to reduce the incidence of car hijackings, a serious crime problem that affects residents of any race or class, but which has proven difficult to counter. Of more than 400 car-jackings in Johannesburg last year, none resulted in prosecution. Under the new project, prosecutors will supervise police investigations of car-jackings to try to improve the quality of the information and evidence gathered in these investigations so that those behind the car-jackings can be brought to justice.

❖ **State/Behavior**

India's National Human Rights Commission (NHRC) - much like human rights commissions in Uganda, Mexico, and other countries - receives complaints related to many forms of human rights abuse. But the overwhelming majority of complaints received by the NHRC are against the police. Special NHRC investigators, (many of them former police officers) look into the claims, determine whether or not there is sufficient evidence to pursue them, and refer them for criminal prosecution. Prosecutors, however, are under no obligation to prosecute these cases, though the NHRC officials say there is a very high rate of compliance. What I believe distinguishes the NHRC from some other human rights commissions is that it also initiates its own research on police violence and misconduct, looking at systemic problem and trends, and makes recommendations for specific police reforms to the government (Perez, forthcoming).

❖ Social/Public Safety

During a crisis in public security in 1992, in which residents of Rio de Janeiro were routinely robbed on the beaches, subjected to car hijackings at traffic intersections, and generally fearful of the rising rate of crime, a broad public constituency appealed to Viva Rio, a non-governmental human rights organization in Rio de Janeiro, to do something about it. In consultation with residents of the poorest communities, or *favelas*, Viva Rio placed "citizen counters' in 20 of these communities. The counters are staffed by law students and social workers who help citizens navigate government and other social services in order to resolve their neighborhood problems, including crime. Viva Rio also set up an anonymous phone hotline for reporting crime, which caused a noticeable increase in the rate of reported crimes since many residents feared retaliation from the accused.   Viva Rio also launched a community policing project in one neighborhood, Copacabana, in partnership with the local police district. The project was well received by both police and citizens, but a change in the state's administration led to the program's early cancellation.

❖ Social/Police Behavior

Under a co-operative agreement with the Hungarian National Police, the Hungarian Helsinki Committee has created the Police Cell Monitoring Project, which authorizes groups of law students and lawyers to make unannounced inspections of police station houses and police cells. They observe what police are doing at the station house, who is being detained, the conditions of detention, and they interview detainees to learn about possible abuses.

By placing some mechanism or another at each level - ones which address the "technical" and "behavioral" aspects of policing - we arrive at a comprehensive system for ensuring that police are both responsive and respectful. But we can still go a step further. Very few accountability structures address both public safety and police conduct, or technical and behavioral police responsibilities. Those that do, I believe, stand to be more effective. Here are three examples of mechanisms that incorporate both things.

Internal: the criteria for a police officer's promotion to a higher rank typically do not include the officer's propensity toward using physical force or the number of civilian complaints that he or she has generated. But once the officer's treatment of citizens, or behavior, becomes critical to his or her career path, the officer will take that responsibility more seriously.

State: We see a crossover between accountability for "technical and behavioral" responsibilities of police in a new but growing class of criminal prosecutions of police, not for mistreating or violating the rights of citizens, but for failing to respond adequately to crime victims. This is, of course, what happened recently in the Stephen Lawrence case in London. In the United States, these suits have most frequently been brought on behalf of domestic violence victims who felt their situations weren't taken seriously by police. Partly because of these cases, some U.S. states have enacted legislation requiring police to make an arrest every time they respond to a domestic violence incident.

Social: The Military Police in the state of São Paulo, Brazil have recently adopted a community policing approach to improve relations between police and the public. The police force came under severe criticism after several police killings in the spring of 1997, three of which were captured on videotape and shown on national television. The public was outraged by the problem of police misconduct, but their criticism also extended to police ineffectiveness, style, militarization, and other "technical" aspects of policing. In response to the criticism, the Military Police established community policing pilot projects in 40 districts, which have been accompanied by retraining, decentralization of command, and other reforms (Mesquita, 1998).

Conclusion

To conclude briefly, what we see from these various examples is that nearly every police accountability mechanism is set up to oversee either how well police provide for public safety or how they treat civilians, but not both. I suggest that these structures could be stronger if they were linked; that is, if police faced the same incentives and the same sanctions, for how well they provide public safety, and for their conduct.

I would just like to reiterate that I don't believe there is any one correct mechanism or combination of mechanisms. The challenge to any democratic society is to create something viable, credible, and effective at each level of the framework I present here. Among the dozen or so countries where I have tried to map out the various accountability mechanisms, like those I present as examples today, I do not come away with any particular model to recommend. But I do believe there is a series of lessons that police, government officials, and citizens of a democracy can take away from our mutual achievements and failures in building a satisfactory police accountability system.

Sources
Davis, Robert C. and Pedro Mateu-Gelabert, "Respectful and Effective Policing: Two Examples in the South Bronx," New York: Vera Institute of Justice, March 1999.

Goldstein, Herman, *Problem – Oriented Policing*. New York: McGraw Hill, 1990.

Mesquita Neto, Paulo de, with Beatriz Stella Affonso, "Policiamento Comunitário: A Experiência em São Paulo," São Paulo: Núcleo de Estudos da Violência da Universidade de São Paulo, September 1998.

Perez, Thomas, "External Governmental Mechanisms of Police Accountability: Three Investigative Structures," *Policing and Society*, forthcoming.

Stone, Christopher E. and Heather H. Ward, "Democratic Policing: A Framework for Action," *Policing and Society*, forthcoming.

The Catalan Police Model

Francesc Guillen[11]

Catalonia and its Spanish context

Catalonia is a small country situated in the North East part of Spain.[12] It covers 31,980 kilometres, corresponding to the Spanish provinces of Barcelona, Girona, Lleida and Tarragona, with the Pyrenees as the northern natural border and the Mediterranean Sea as the eastern boundary. Catalonia has six million inhabitants. Our language is Catalan which comes from Latin, as do Spanish, French and Italian.

The Spanish Constitutional Framework

After Franco's dictatorship (1939 - 1975) that removed any kind of self-government, the restoration of democracy (namely the Spanish Constitution of 1978) established a sort of federal state with special powers for what it calls "historical nationalities" (mainly Catalonia, Galicia and the Basque Country). That implied the creation of what we call Autonomous Communities with the powers established by their respective constitutions. Some of these constitutions (particularly the ones for the Basque Country, Navarra and Catalonia) gave the possibility of creating police forces that were dependent on the Autonomous Governments.

---

[11] Francesc Guillen is Head of Research at the Police School of Catalonia, and has held this post since May 1992. Having studied law - both comparative and constitutional - he has lectured in the Department of Constitutional Law at the Autonomous University of Barcelona since 1989. Mr Guillen has a large number of academic publications to his name, specialising in police and constitutional law, and he has acted as an expert police adviser for the Council of Europe in Central America and in Georgia.

[12] Actually, historically some of the territories of the South of France (those being closest to the Spanish border) also belonged to Catalonia. Nowadays, they are a part of French territory and have no autonomy.

The Autonomous System established by the Spanish Constitution of 1978 has a lot of similarities with federal systems like the German or the American ones. But it has one strong difference: not all the Autonomous Communities have the same powers. That is why not all of them can have their own police force. One should think of a decentralised system, but with different levels of powers.

Furthermore, there is a third level of autonomy - the municipal level. The constitution acknowledges local autonomy and as a result of that, municipalities have been given powers to have their own police forces. Catalan Home Rule gave our self-governing institutions (we call them "*Generalitat de Catalunya*") powers to co-ordinate municipal police forces (the powers included police training, monitoring and standardising technology and information systems, basic common regulations, etc).

So, there are three levels of government in Spain:

a)   **State - Spanish Home Office - two state police forces:**
  - National Police
  - Civil Guard

b)   **Autonomous:**
  - All the Autonomous Communities have powers to co-ordinate municipal police forces.
  - Seven of them have powers to create their own police forces (though only three out of seven have actually created them - the Basque Country, Navarra and Catalonia as mentioned above).

c)   **Municipal:**
  - Any municipality having more than 5,000 inhabitants (10,000 in Catalonia) has the power to create a new municipal police force. Nowadays, in Catalonia alone, there exist 180 municipal police forces, ranging in size between 2,500 officers (Barcelona city) to 10 or 15 officers (some small villages having established their police force prior to the population requirement being enacted).

Development of the Catalan Police Model

Although Catalan Home Rule was enacted at the end of 1979, and came into force on 1st January 1980, establishing that the *Generalitat* had powers to create its own police force, it took a long time to develop this power. First of all, the Catalan Parliament created the Police Force (from the existing body of *Mossos d'Esquadra*[13]) in 1983, but it started to work very slowly with some police officers working in very specialised areas, such as juvenile justice, gambling, public order and prison oversight. Time showed the need to develop Catalan Home Rule to a greater degree, that is to say, to transform *Mossos d'Esquadra* into the ordinary police in Catalonia. Finally, agreement was reached (on 17th October 1994) and the Catalan Security Council (*Junta de Seguretat*), made up of representatives from the *Generalitat* and the Central Spanish Government, decided to develop *Mossos d'Esquadra* into the ordinary police of Catalonia over a period of eight years (later it was lengthened to ten).[14]. This involves the gradual substitution of the Civil Guard and National Police by the *Mossos d'Esquadra*. This process started in 1994, it will continue county by county and will be completed by the year 2005.

These were the original provisions. Recently, there have been some changes. The most important one is that *Mossos d'Esquadra* will probably be starting their deployment in the Barcelona area in the year 2001. Consequently, the rest of the phases will be delayed.

---

[13] Our police (the "Police of the *Generalitat*" or the *Mossos d'Esquadra* - you can use both names) has deep roots. It was created for the first time in 1721 as a police force to fight against bandits in some rural areas of Catalonia. Historians say that they were the first police force, in the modern sense, in Spain. Actually, it is true that when the Civil Guard was created (1843), they copied some things from the *Mossos d'Esquadra* (such as the internal code of conduct - the '*Cartilla*'). Whenever Catalonia secured autonomy, the *Mossos d'Esquadra* were always under the direction of the *Generalitat* (which is the name of our institutions of Government) - that means during the autonomy we had in the second Spanish Republic (1931 - 1939), and since the arrival of democracy and autonomy in the current period.

[14] The main factor to facilitate the agreement between the State and the *Generalitat* was the fact that the Spanish Socialist Party lost its overall majority in 1993, needing the support from other parties (namely, the Catalan Ruling Nationalist Parties). In the 1996 elections the Popular Party did not have an overall majority either, so they also needed the support of the Nationalist Parties. Thus, the Agreement was respected.

When the *Mossos d'Esquadra* take on a new county, most Civil Guard and National Police Officers withdraw, just leaving a few to be responsible for state powers. Eventually there will only remain a few hundred of these in Catalonia.

The final Catalan Policing system will integrate three kinds of police forces:

(a)   Police of the *Generalitat / Mossos d'Esquadra*

These are considered to be the ordinary police in Catalonia. They answer to the Ministry of Interior of the *Generalitat* and have full powers for: the protection of people and properties; maintaining public order; surveillance and protection of authorities and buildings of the *Generalitat* ; surveillance of public places; protection of public demonstrations and the maintenance of public order and crowd control; giving assistance in cases of accidents and disasters and taking part in the development of emergency plans; protection of citizens' safety; crime prevention; the enforcement of legislation enacted by Catalan Parliament and Government, with special care in the field of environment, goods and properties belonging to cultural heritage and private police; the enforcement of state legislation that is in force in Catalonia; and crime investigation.

All crimes except some remain within the remit of the National Police and the Civil Guard. The crimes remaining under state jurisdiction are the following ones: crimes connected to state security; crimes against the King, the Queen, the Prince or the separation of powers; coin forgery; serious fraud that can alter prices of the market affecting the general economy of the state; drug trafficking, fraud with food and medicines if they are committed by groups that work outside the Catalan territory; terrorism; crime committed by state authorities and members of state police forces; other crimes under the jurisdiction of the Supreme Court or the *Audencia Nacional*.

(b)   The National Police and Civil Guard

They work in the framework of the state powers such as we have just seen. One should add customs, border control and other similar powers directly linked to state powers.

(c)   **180 Municipal Police Forces (current figures)**

These work in the areas of traffic and administrative policing, and some tasks traditionally included in the concept of community policing (quality of life, assisting citizens etc).

Instruments for co-operation

Obviously, if we are thinking of three different levels of government having their own police forces and one of them having two different ones, co-operation is the first problem to be faced. Since everybody is concerned by the risk of lack of co-ordination (in terms of security), several instruments for co-operation have been designed:

(a)   **The Catalan Council for Safety (established by the Constitution)**

This body is composed of representatives from the central state and the *Generalitat* (50% each). Its aim is to agree on the different phases of the *Mossos d'Esquadra* development and co-ordinate state and *Generalitat* police forces. Actually, this organ has not been too successful, since for almost fifteen years it has been used by the central government to stop and delay the *Mossos d'Esquadra* development. Only when central government needed political support in the Spanish parliament was an agreement achieved. Moreover, it has never been a true tool for co-operation. It is true that the level of co-ordination between Spanish and Catalan police forces is very acceptable nowadays, but it is not due to the work done by the Catalan Council for Safety. It has been due to other forms of co-operation.

(b)   **Municipal Safety Council**

In all municipalities with a municipal police force this organ must exist. It is chaired by the mayor, and all police forces working in the municipality have to be represented. The aims are to co-ordinate the different police services working there, plan crime prevention strategies, etc. Although they have not been built up in all municipalities where they should have been created, wherever they exist they help in the co-ordination of all actors in the field of policing.

(c)   "Co-ordination Rooms"

These are places where there are representatives from the different police forces working in the territory. Their aim is sharing information related to policing (mainly crime investigation). There exists a "Co-ordination Room" one in Barcelona and one more in every Catalan province. The current experience is entirely positive. They have been extremely useful in avoiding loss of information and in effectively building upon the resources of different police services. Everybody has understood that they all need each other. Since the *Mossos d'Esquadra* are going to become the ordinary police in Catalonia, they will receive most of the police information in Catalonia. So, the National Police and the Civil Guard will have to deal with the *Mossos* if they want to have that information. Equally, if the Mossos d'Esquadra want to have information about what has happened in the past or about what is happening in the rest of the state, they need to get it from the National Police and Civil Guard. So, co-ordination is in the interests of all involved.

(d)   Security Policies Council

This exists at the state level. It should be chaired by the Spanish Home Secretary and includes all Autonomous Communities' Home Secretaries[15]. Actually, it has never worked due to the fact that it tries to combine very different things, such as Communities with their own police service and others without. This organ gathers people with very different interests, and this is probably the reason for its failure.

Apart from these official mechanisms, there are many forms of co-operation at the informal level, usually through bilateral contacts.

Reasons for raising our own police force

There have been a lot of arguments in Spain about the fact that the Catalan Government decided to create and develop a new police service. With such a

---

[15] Although not all Autonomous Communities have their own police service, all of them have powers to co-ordinate municipal police services. That is why they all have a role in this organism.

complicated policing system, one might think that other solutions should have been sought. That is why it is important to discuss again the main reason that led to the creation and the development of a new force.

First of all, it was considered a normal consequence of the decision to establish Catalan self-government. A country that is self-governing should also have its own police service.

Secondly, there was an opportunity to provide a better service. For example:

1. A new police service could offer a service in the country's language. Traditionally Spanish police officers working in Catalonia have not been able to speak Catalan, which is the indigenous language.

2. A new police service could take care of the citizens' needs better than the pre-existing ones due to different factors:

*   **Involving police in community.** New police officers were more acceptable since they would belong to the country and they would not be just passers-by, spending some time in Catalonia before being sent elsewhere in the Spanish territory. New police officers would know people's concerns since these would be, in some cases, their neighbour's concerns.

*   **Involving community in policing**. Traditionally the Catalan population has looked, not only on the police service, but also on the Civil Service overall, as something alien to our tradition. Public administration had been something organised by Madrid (and from there) and was not of much appeal in Catalonia. It was agreed that if there was any chance of attracting local youngsters to the police service it was through something new which had no links with the past. In this sense, the creation of a new police service has succeeded, ensuring that a lot of Catalans have applied to join the *Mossos d'Esquadra*.

Apart from that, a new police force could raise people's interest in policing - encouraging them to talk about policing needs, their concerns, and facilitate their participation in the design of policing policies etc.

At this point, it is very important to clarify that: by saying what has just been said, I do not mean in any sense to suggest that the Civil Guard and National Police do not care about people's concerns, or that they are not democratic. They, of course, are democratic. A lot of resources have been used to change the pre-existing police forces; a lot of training has been carried out. By no means would it be fair to say that their standards, speaking in general terms, are undemocratic.

The main problem is that they have a heavy history hanging over them and this cannot be changed overnight. It is easier with a new police force. The old police officers, although they learn how to work in democracy, can retain those attitudes from the past.[16] Professionally speaking, however, they are good and I would say that it will not be easy for the *Mossos d'Esquadra* to equalise them.

I would also like to state that they are not hated by the Catalan population, since they have behaved well in recent years. The key point is that if you ask the Catalan population to choose between their police and the state police, they would choose the former.

Raised expectations and current trends

Although Catalans remain sceptical about the police (you cannot reverse such an ingrained attitude in a very short time), a lot of them have understood the message of change. It means that they study the police and policing and are ready to tell them their worries, their needs, etc. But, moreover, they now understand that they will be consulted when planning policing strategies and that they will be able to criticise what they do not like.

Now that the *Mossos d'Esquadra* are the ordinary police in the north-east of Catalonia (coverage of the western region will be complete by the end of the year), promises have been respected from the police service's point of view. They have had monthly contacts with most of the permanent and stable

---

[16] According to the terms used by another speaker (Ralph Crawshaw) in yesterday's lecture, one could say that they are very good in the technical field, but they sometimes fail in the behavioural one.

associations in that area (shop owners, neighbours, hunters, migrants etc.), with all the existing municipalities, schools, etc. Furthermore, they attend special meetings when there is any particular problem which requires listening to the concerned parties. Finally, they have created press services which offer a daily service of information to the media.

After such an extraordinary effort, most police officers thought that people would be very satisfied, almost applauding them for their openness and willingness to work with the community. Nevertheless, it has not been entirely smooth. The population was promised that it was the moment that they would be able to give their opinion about police and policing, and they have taken that message very seriously. They have come and have said what they like and what not, in a very clear way. Never before had our population been so critical of the State Police[17]. Never before had the media criticised so bitterly the former police forces. That situation has created a great degree of disappointment amongst the police. They feel themselves unfairly treated in comparison to the previous situation. Nowadays, some of them are reluctant even to deal with the media at all.

What are we going to do to go forward? Are we going to change our strategy? Absolutely not, we are taking a risk on change. We wanted people to be involved in policing. We (at least some of us) believed in that message. The current situation is not so surprising if studied calmly. In a democratic society, pluralism is normality. That is to say, usually (and luckily) not everybody likes the same things, discussions are frequent and consequently, conflicts form part of daily life. So, it is normal that, if we called people to tell us what they wanted in police terms, they did just that. It is also normal that some people do not like what the police do. Yet we must also recognise that it is very

---

[17] There is a very interesting anecdote defining perfectly some people's attitudes towards *Mossos d'Esquadra*. After being deployed for some days in the first Catalan county (Ossona), a citizen phoned the Chief Constable's office to complain about a police car parking in a forbidden place in a very narrow street in the city centre. The Chief Constable (who was born in that city) answered: "Well, Spanish National Police officers have been parking there for forty years and nobody complained about that. You should give us some time to adapt to the new situation". The citizen on the phone answered "But you are here because we want you to be here. We were obliged to put up with them, whether we liked it or not. You cannot behave in the way they did - you are dependent upon us". The Chief Constable was very shocked by this and said "Yes sir, you are entirely right. I apologise for that - it will not happen again".

difficult to change. We have to encourage our police officers to cope with the new reality. They have to realise that normality is not thinking that things will always be more or less the same. Instead they must get used to dealing with discussion and controversy. There is no possibility of going back: the challenge is one of developing a capacity to face public demand, satisfy it where possible, and learn to accept public disagreements about policing. The current situation needs to be seen not as a failure but as a major success.

The Illusion of Consent:
Community Policing or Policed Communities?

Phil Scraton[18]

Hillsborough and After: A Cause for Concern

t is a decade since 96 men, women and children were crushed to death on the terraces as a top soccer match kicked-off at Hillsborough stadium in England. 400 were hospitalised, 700 injured and thousands traumatised. The stadium's safety certificate was 10 years out-of-date, the venue was in a poor state, stewarding disorganised, and medical facilities and equipment minimal. Over the years crowd management and safety had been neglected as clubs and the police put resources into containment, control and regulation. The 'mind-set' was hooliganism and disorder.

Minutes before kick-off, the South Yorkshire Police match commander ordered the opening of an exit gate to relieve congestion at the turnstiles. Over 2,000 fans entered, unstewarded and unpoliced, walking down a steep tunnel opposite the gate and unwittingly into the rear of two already packed central pens. Pens like cattle pens – fences at the front and sides. Police failure to seal off the tunnel and divert fans to the half-empty side pens made the fatal crush inevitable; there was no escape.

In the immediate aftermath the bereaved and survivors looked on as their loved ones were demonised in the media and in police submissions to the inquiries. As the South Yorkshire Police sought to deny their negligence, it emerged that while the disaster was happening the match commander lied to Football Association officials that fans had forced entry causing an "inrush"

---

[18] Professor Phil Scraton is Professor of Criminology and Director of the Centre for Studies in Crime and Social Justice, Edge Hill University College. He has written several books including: *The State of the Police*, Pluto; *Law, Order and the Authoritarian State*, Open University Press and, most recently, *Hillsborough: The Truth*, Mainstream.

into the ground. The lie was broadcast around the world. Later in the day the coroner took the unprecedented step of ordering blood alcohol levels to be taken from all who died, including young children. Police officers used off-the-record briefings to allege that fans had stolen from and sexually abused the dead and urinated on police officials attempting resuscitation. The South Yorkshire police version was they had done their best in the face of drunken, violent and ticketless fans determined to force entry.

Within days of the Hillsborough disaster a Home Office inquiry was announced, under Lord Justice Taylor, and the West Midlands police conducted the criminal investigation and serviced the inquiry. The bereaved and survivors expected that given the breadth and depth of the inquiries the 'truth' of Hillsborough would emerge and those responsible would face prosecution. This expectation solidified when Taylor found that the "main reason" for the disaster was a "failure of police control". The decision to open the exit gate without sealing off the tunnel had been "a blunder of the first magnitude". He condemned senior officers for their ineptitude on the day and their behaviour at the inquiry. Despite Taylor's findings, the Director of Public Prosecutions decided there was insufficient evidence to prosecute any officer. Although the Police Complaints Authority recommended disciplinary action against the match commander and his assistant it was abandoned when the former retired on the grounds of ill-health.

In 1998, following eight years of painstaking research, it emerged that the South Yorkshire Police had created an unprecedented procedure within the force to review and alter the police testimonies initially gathered. Immediately after the disaster, officers were instructed not to write in their pocket books. Days later they were told to provide written 'recollections' of the day, not confined to the 'facts' but including feelings and opinion. They were advised, in writing, that their recollections were not formal statements, were 'privileged' documents and were not for submission to the investigation or inquiry.

Once collected, the officers' recollections were sent to the force solicitors and then returned to a specially designated South Yorkshire police team with recommendations for 'review' and 'alteration'. The team then visited their colleagues throughout the force gaining their signatures to the amended recollections and forwarded the documents as reconstructed statements to the criminal investigation and the Taylor inquiry team.   The West Midlands investigators, the Treasury solicitor and Lord Justice Taylor knew of and accepted the process. Effectively, the mass of evidence gathered from the hundreds of officers on duty was altered to remove criticism of senior officers while retaining negative comment and opinion on the behaviour of the fans. It was a process not derived from the discretion of a few officers but one that originated at the highest level, became institutionalised and involved the outside investigating and inquiry teams. Yet, for nearly a decade, it remained hidden from the bereaved and their lawyers.

Liberal Democratic Principles

Whatever distinctions are drawn within and between liberal democratic theories of the relationship between the state and the police, five key principles remain consistent. They date back to the political debates which contextualised the 1829 Metropolitan Police Act and the formation of the 'New Police', preceding the full franchise in Britain by nearly a century. Their roots lay with late 18th Century liberal reformers such as Colquhoun and the Fielding brothers.

First was the assertion that the police were no more than *citizens-in-uniform*, enforcing 'our' laws on 'our' behalf. The powers held lawfully by those appointed to the office of constable did not place the police above the law; they were citizens subject to the rule of law. Related to this principle was the second: that the police were *of the community*, reflecting its composition and its interests.

The third principle emphasised the *neutrality* and *impartiality* of the police. This recognised that while conflict was inevitable within a pluralist society of competing interests, once the boundaries of acceptable conflict had been drawn, they would require policing. And so the police were represented as the arbiters of social conflict, the 'thin blue line', devoid of institutional or professional self-interest.

Fourth, was the clear presumption that a society with complex rules and regulations required a representative police presence. Thus, in establishing a regulatory agenda for crime and its prevention, for crime detection, industrial conflict and the maintenance of public order, policing was by *consent*. The police were not only the 'keepers of the peace' through their operational powers, they were the 'guardians of consensus' through their operational discretion.

Finally, the police were *accountable*, both *legally* and *politically*. That they were subject to the law meant that the primary check on the use and abuse of their powers was legal - the full force of prosecution. They were also constrained by the force disciplinary code, which regulated practices not necessarily covered by the criminal code. Both processes were governed by a supposedly independent procedure for investigating complaints. Complaints against the police were investigated by the police, although an 'independent' body was eventually appointed to oversee the investigation of serious complaints. Alongside this process were police 'watch committees', later to become local police authorities, whose brief was to secure an "adequate and efficient" police force for the area. The 'modern' triangle of political accountability, with the exception of the Metropolitan Police, became the Home Secretary (national government), Police Authorities (local councillors and magistrates) and Chief Constables.

In less than 100 years the principles of civil policing had become embedded in official discourse. The 1929 Royal Commission, for example, claimed that the British police had "never been recognised either *in law* or *by tradition* as a force distinct from the *general body of citizens*". The guiding principle being that a police officer "in the view of the *common law*, is a person paid to perform, as a matter of duty, acts which he [sic] might have done voluntarily". Nearly 60 years later, in 1983, as the Merseyside Police attempted to rescue its battered reputation with its working-class and black communities it proclaimed "two very important advantages" over other police forces throughout the world: "Firstly, that it was founded on a tradition of *common law* – law that *evolved naturally* to meet the needs of the people – and, secondly that its officers are drawn *from the community*, performing their duties *on behalf of us all*. The job of the police is therefore to uphold *our own self-imposed rules*".

According to Robert Mark, former Metropolitan Police Commissioner, that the police are answerable to the Rule of Law and "not under the mantle of government" makes them "the *least powerful*, the *most accountable* and therefore the *most acceptable* police force in the world". His successor, David McNee, reaffirmed that the "original instructions" for policing established in

1829 "made it clear that the old tradition of policing from *within the community,* with the *consent of the community* was the *guiding principle* of the new system".

Establishing a Critical Analysis

A critical analysis of policing presents a contrasting historical and theoretical account. Policing in Britain, it has to be remembered, was not a product of democracy. It preceded the democratic process by nearly a century. The New Police not only regulated communities which were politically and economically marginalised, they protected the interests of an established and consolidating order derived in structural inequalities - of early capitalism, of patriarchy and of imperialism. Institutionally, policing functioned to maintain the *status quo,* emphasising the significance of certain crimes over others, of the threats of civil disorder, of industrial conflict, of suffragism and of colonial rule.

Far from being a static, monolithic and impartial agency of neutral law enforcement, police work has always been a *process* responsive to changes in social, political and economic conditions. Over time this has led to *diversification* and *specialisation* reflecting the range of tasks and duties expected of operational policing. Yet policing, cannot escape society's *structural contradictions* and *inequalities* and the inherent confrontations between the police and the policed over what constitutes 'unacceptable' or 'criminal' behaviour. Consequently, crime or disorder are not consistent, universally accepted categories. Changes in the political economy, shifts in the structural relations of advanced capitalism, patriarchy or neo-colonialism, bring changes in what is *defined* as crime and changes in the levels and intensity of industrial, political and urban conflict.

Police intervention is inherently *political* and illustrative of dominant power relations and structural social divisions. To portray the police as the 'thin blue line' or neutral arbiters in external, social conflict is naïve; a simplistic and decontextualised version of the tradition of policing within the British state at home or abroad. That the police are, in some mystical way, 'above politics' operating outside the inherent, structural conflicts of classism, racism, sectarianism, sexism, is plausible yet illusory. The targeting of identifiable groups by the police – the deployment of 'saturation tactics' in selected neighbourhoods – has its root in a long history of 'differential policing'. It is not simply a matter of attitudinal discrimination - the isolated actions of individual officers - but the regular, institutionalised use of negative images incorporated into the general ideology of police operations and practice, which then become a central part of the political management of communities.

'Tiered' Policing

Throughout the history of contemporary policing the claim that the police operate as a 'local' force, responding operationally in *policies*, *priorities* and *practices* to the identified needs of communities, has persisted. Established as part of local government, under Home Office supervision and centralised inspection, police forces have each developed their own identities within their set boundaries. Specialisation and diversification, however, together with the complexities of policing crime, public order and industrial conflict, has led to the consolidation of regional and national policing initiatives with increased cooperation across local force boundaries. While local policing sets objectives around violent street crime, burglary, crime prevention, high community visibility and prompt response to calls, national initiatives include the National Crime Squad and the National Criminal Intelligence Service.

Also operating at a national level are the security services, notably the Special Branch. While often having minimal contact with the UK's police forces on the ground, the security services have developed strong links internationally. Since the early 1990s Europeanisation has led to inter-state collaboration including cross-border controls, immigration, anti-terrorism, organised crime and the 'war on drugs'. These policies, derived in international agreements but debated neither in member states' parliaments nor at local government levels, stand outside any recognisable form of political accountability. Yet, professionally, through the Association of Chief Police Officers, the police have significant direct formulative and organisational involvement in cross-border initiatives. It is precisely this form of development which has led to criticisms of the Association as being relatively autonomous of local and/or national government in operational policy and strategy matters.

What this 'tripartite' structure (local, national, European) of policing amounts to is *tiered policing*; different forms of police work operating at quite distinct levels of intervention. It raises questions, however, about the effectiveness of the checks and balances on *police powers*. Guided by the twin principles of *reasonable force* and *reasonable suspicion,* the use of *lawful discretion* in the use of police powers has been governed by three distinct but related processes of accountability discussed above: legal, organisational and political. Much has been written to demonstrate the difficulties associated with police complaints procedures and the failure of the Police Complaints Authority and the criminal courts to secure convictions or disciplinary outcomes. From the early 1980s there has been considerable controversy over the effectiveness of political accountability. The research shows a systematic erosion of the powers of elected representatives resulting in a *democratic deficit* at all levels of policing within the UK.

'Total' Policing

In the context of local policing in Britain much has been made since Scarman of *community policing*. This has not only meant a more visible, 'on-the-beat' strategy of community police work, but has involved the police in a range of proactive, preventative measures. These include: neighbourhood watch; community safety; schools liaison; victim support; target hardening; local intelligence gathering. In developing multi-agency strategies the emphasis has been ostensibly on community participation and consultation through community forums and police-community liaison committees. Community policing, however, has been heavily criticised as a sophisticated form of community surveillance with civilian volunteers seen as small-scale informants. Consultation is derided as a one-way street.

Problems with community policing have been exacerbated by the consolidation and normalisation of *paramilitary* strategies within UK forces. Previously visible primarily in the North of Ireland, paramilitarism within UK forces has been normalised in resources, equipment and training. It brings with it a set of preconceived attitudes and approaches to certain communities and specific individuals. Proffered as 'last resort' policing, it can too quickly be deployed as a 'first response'. The difficulty lies in the day-to-day transition between the 'velvet glove' of community policing and the 'iron fist' of paramilitary policing. This not only is a problem for those policed, it poses a serious dichotomy for the police officers involved. For Sir Kenneth Newman, former RUC Chief Constable and Metropolitan Police Commissioner, there was no contradiction. He saw the compatibility of community policing and paramilitary responses within the overarching principle of *total policing*. A principle which spoke for itself.

For Newman, total policing constituted *targeting, surveillance, regulation* and *intervention,* regardless of whether specific operations were derived in community-based strategies or hardline initiatives. The constant theme being: "honest citizens have nothing to fear". Total policing, however, suggests a social order in which *disciplined subjects* live and relate within *monitored communities*. The normalisation of once special powers together with the expansion of computer-based surveillance technology has secured the vision of a totally policed society. This is connected to hard-line authoritarian initiatives 'plumbed in' to established forms of *differential policing*. The 'targets' reflect the political economy of marginalisation, social exclusion and institutionalised discrimination. When Scarman refused to accept that racism within the Metropolitan Police was institutionalised he legitimated priorities and practices which had long infected the policing of black communities. It took another 18 years, and a sustained campaign by the family and supporters of Stephen Lawrence, to establish what had long been apparent in Britain's black communities; the police were, and remain, institutionally racist.

As with sectarianism, racism is an expression of marginalisation and exclusion. Others include: unemployment and poverty; misogyny and homophobia; childhood and youth; culture and belief. While publicly expressed as ideologies, both in official discourse and institutional practices, they are material – political and economic – realities. They were central to the 'Thatcherite project'. Now, the prevailing climate reflects the authoritarian inheritance of Thatcherism to the extent that New Labour's current 'law and order' legislation and its justification represents a seamless transition from the policies of the New Right. As Diane Abbott, MP recently remarked, the Home Secretary, Jack Straw, is no more than Michael Howard, his predecessor, "in drag". The 'policing' and regulatory emphases within a clearly political agenda are: an 'underclass' culpable for its own exclusion; the breakdown of the 'family'; the growth of 'persistent young offending'. They are supported by analysis and explanations derived in a pseudo-scientific construction of individual and community pathologies and promulgated by self-styled 'ethical socialists'.

This political climate has inspired strategies of crime prevention, based on early intervention, surveillance, targeting and 'zero tolerance' of petty crime and antisocial behaviour. It is supported by a rhetoric combining the 'protection' of 'vulnerable' individuals and groups, the 'fear of crime' within communities, and the construction of 'high risk' potential offenders. The civil restraining orders within the draconian 1998 Crime and Disorder Act amount to a politics of criminalisation which, along with electronic tagging, widen the 'net' of crime and extend the reach of punishment in the community. In the provision of local crime audits, on which the now statutory multi-agency strategies for reducing crime and disorder have been based, the police have played a defining role. While local authorities and other public bodies are obliged by law to participate, the police in practice assume the role of lead agency. It is to be expected that legislation resembling the 1998 Act will be introduced in the North of Ireland.

Police Accountability is a Rights Issue

When political commentators, campaign groups and academics talk of policing in *transitional* states, the usual context is one in which previously unrepresentative state forms are moving to social democracy. Often this involves the transition of policing from being a militarised function of direct oppression to that of a civil function of 'peace' and its maintenance. What this paper has argued, however, is that even in 'advanced' social democracies there are dichotomies which demonstrate difficulties in resolving the politics of policing: the police as a *service* set against the police as a *force*; a *duty of care* set against a *dynamic of control*; the *illusion of consent* set against the *reality of coercion*.

What the opening, brief excursion into the complex Hillsborough case starkly reveals is that it does not take institutionalised racism or sectarianism to create the context in which police and criminal justice agencies fail in their investigations, distort evidence and marginalise victims. In this South Yorkshire tragedy, deep political and ideological assumptions, coupled with professional self-interest and survival, combined to demonise, deny and neutralise the 'truth'. In so doing justice was undermined and human rights cast aside.

How the police are experienced by individuals or within communities depends significantly on shared police assumptions about location, identity, status and reputation. Policing does not occur in a political vacuum. It is not simply attitudinal, altered by better recruitment, training and management, but is profoundly ideological. The shared assumptions of negative reputation are deeply institutionalised. As the Association of Chief Police Officers has confirmed its relative autonomy from local and national government, so the denial of effective political accountability and meaningful community consultation has been realised.

Within Britain the removal of the democratic deficit and the transition to open, fair, transparent and accountable policing remains unresolved. There has to be informed political and public debate around tiered policing with operational police policies and practices subjected to the rigours of consultation and accountability. In establishing strategies and priorities the guiding principle has to be respect for and protection of human rights.

Management of Change

Zelda Holtzman[19]

Thank you, good afternoon. I am very aware of the fact that we have had quite an intense session earlier on and I am sure there are a number of questions still hanging. I hope to be addressing some of those questions in the address I am about to give.

Firstly, thanks to CAJ. I am very privileged to be part of this conference since it serves as a reminder of similar processes we went through in South Africa prior to our first democratic elections in 1994. I am therefore convinced that I will not only share with you our experiences of the transformation of the South African police, but that we will also learn from your current experiences.

Transforming the South African police has not been an easy task. The South African Police or the SAP as we knew it, was characterised as a paramilitary force which used brutal measures to ensure compliance with the apartheid laws. It was therefore alienated from the majority of our population. Although black people were to be found in that institution, they mainly occupied the lower ranks. The surrogate police agencies in the bantustans consisted of a predominantly black membership who in turn were badly trained and unacceptable to the very black communities from which they came. Now this was an institution which had to transform itself to an agency which is representative of the people they serve, which is sensitive to the needs of the community and generally to police in such a manner that would reflect the spirit of our new Constitution. The immediate question arises as to whether the police, given its make-up and history, has the capacity to transform itself. A follow-up question will be whether there is a critical mass within the police to drive forward the change process. To both questions I will answer no. And in

---

[19] Zelda Lynn Holtzman is Assistant Commissioner of the South African Police Service, and has headed up their National Equity Component since February 1996. Now director of the Change Management Team that was responsible for facilitating and developing processes for the transformation of the South African Police Service, Ms Holtzman came from a community work background previously. Before joining the South African Police as a lateral entrant, she was involved in training police in community policing, and she both lectured on and designed community policing programmes and projects.

this lies the weakness of our transformation processes. The few of us who acted as change agents basically had to go through innovative, creative and sometimes downright manipulative measures to ensure some movement in the direction of change.

The above predicament was further exacerbated by the fact that there was no clear direction from the political office as to what change or transformation meant. This was only clarified towards the end of 1998 in the White Paper of Safety and Security. So sectors of police and some other role players, including the Secretariat for Safety and Security and the police unions had to find a match between immediate needs such as representativity, community orientated problem-solving policing and service provision, where total instability and at times near anarchy existed. These were indeed difficult times with none of the stake holders being satisfied, and a police management who, at times, appeared intransigent.

For the problem has not been in the definition of police transformation, but rather in the definition of policing itself. It has often been assumed that you should continue with police functions in a "normal way" without questioning what normal is. Some argue the that normal is the way they do it in Britain or Canada. I'm not so sure.. I am very glad that Phil (Speaker: Phil Scraton) raised the question as to "whose law and what order?", since it really is about policing objectives. In a divided society, there definitely would be different types of 'order'. What would be normal for one community might be totally abnormal for another, and one has to take that on board, so that you don't get a force that would in its own mind, try to establish an 'order' which is totally out of sync with the communities it serves.

It is essential therefore that we clarify the objectives of policing. In South Africa the objective of policing as stipulated in our Constitution and Police Act, is to bring about and maintain safety and security. This is an extremely important shift from "the law and order" paradigm. Given this focus, it is unquestionable that the police cannot meet this objective on its own, and certainly not use the same methods to achieve these noble objectives. So let us stretch this position a bit further. If the objective of policing is safety and security, who then are the guardians of safety and security? And does the police, if you assume that they are the sole guardians of safety and security, do they have the capacity to carry out that mandate to bring about safety and security? Indeed, I think that anyone who has any experience of policing would immediately argue that the police as an institution should never hold monopoly rights to policing.

In this equation of policing, organised, empowered community agencies hold the balance to the services which will make communities safer places to live. I particularly mention organised and empowered since they mean different things and because I think that often "communities" are constructs which exists in the minds of those who need partners to rubber-stamp authoritarian positions. If you want to do that, you could always find a community to support you. Organised and empowered communities who have mandates (not necessarily formal) from communities they serve and represent.

Other agencies in civil society, and indeed in our context, proved to be very key in the establishment of safety and security. These structures, organic or inorganic, contributed significantly towards peace and stability. These structures of self-regulation - be it community justice, community courts, committees, bloc committees, and so on, made their mark nearly despite the state of policing. The mandates given to these structures were historical and could be found in the articulation of a unified position. This should be seen against a police institution which to date still does not speak with a unified voice and is still not representative of the people we serve. A very interesting question faces us in the future. If the police is seen to be doing its job and delivering on safety and security, would the same mandate for civil society still exist or would it be withdrawn?

There is another agency which is very important in this equation of safety and security provision - private policing. About three years ago or so, private security firms and private security personnel outnumbered state policing by five to one, and this ratio is now possibly close to seven or eight to one at this point. This growth should be strictly monitored if we want to get a handle on transforming policing. As much as it could aid community safety it could, by the same token, negatively affect safety provision because of its profit motive and lack of accountability. I will not elaborate on this aspect of policing since it probably requires a paper on its own, and I will not be able to do justice to the topic in the limited time given.

There is also the "other" category in this equation of policing - i.e. the sector which you cannot quite define, but which nonetheless play an important role in securing safety for communities.   In our case, it might be traditional policing - chieftains who have their own areas of authority, tradition, convention and customs.   They have acquired for themselves certain roles and responsibilities in as far as the maintenance of order is concerned.   But the "other" could also mean the churches.   In some rural areas you find that the church has quite an extensive jurisdiction, particularly when it comes to juvenile problems.   However, it also could include extreme groups of vigilantes who impose upon communities some form of regulation.   There is a particular case in the Western Cape, for example, where a group called *People Against Gangsterism and Drug Abuse* (PAGAD) have taken the law unto themselves. They would seem to be yet another agency of enforcement, totally armed and trained, also conducting activities which do not necessarily bring about order, but rather disorder.   I think that before you look at policing outcomes one has to take cognisance of all these factors that impact upon it before making the argument that we should just "get back to normal policing and things will be the same again."

My argument is that if you concentrate solely on policing then you are missing the point.   If however, you look at all those other factors and agencies influencing policing, you also have to look at the way in which the transformation of those agencies, particularly in civil society, would impact upon the transformation of the police. I don't think it has to be a negative relationship, or one that would be an antagonistic contradiction between the two.

Let me try and return to the transformation of the South Africa Police Service. If you speak to people in the top management about what transformation entails, they would tell you three things.   They will all agree that transformation involves amalgamation, rationalisation and change'.   Now what it actually means was that you had one dominant police agency, the South African police, and alongside it, you had the surrogate police agencies. The Constitution made provision for the South African Police Service to amalgamate with all the surrogate agencies, and also to integrate with sections of the military wings of the liberation movement, and today this constitutes the South African Police Service.   Essentially, the concept of 'amalgamation' was a merger of police agencies plus some non-statutory bodies; it was this merger that constituted the amalgamation process.

The 'rationalisation' entailed the development of structures to contain all these amalgamated bodies into one. To achieve this, a new structure had to be drafted to which members were appointed after applying for posts. This was quite new to the police who never previously had to apply and compete for posts. But now, jobs were advertised and they had to present their CV's, had to be short-listed etc. It was at that point that a number of people just couldn't accept the changes. There was a very deep sense of entitlement based on patronage and apartheid logic. The new system challenged all of this. The following sentiments were silently expressed: "how could you now be competing with those other people?" " where did they come from?" "This is our force," etc. Some people couldn't handle that change. Many of the senior managers left because of an inability to compete with people whom they considered to be inferior to themselves. If, as a result of the competition they were thrown out, it would be such a let-down for the Afrikaner white male ego. So, that was one of the problems that we faced. But nonetheless it assisted us with the rationalisation process.

So, that was amalgamation and rationalisation. Now if one was to focus on 'change' and you ask senior managers what does change entail, you would get lots of different answers. There is an assumption that change is those things that are purely symbolic. So, a lot of emphasis was placed on changing the police uniforms, which indeed we did, on changing the rank structure, which we did (from fourteen ranks to ten): that was significant for a lot of people. We did away with some of the military ranks and also changed the insignia so that instead of having a castle on the shoulder representing the colonial conquest, we have now changed it to a hexagon. I don't know what the new insignia actually means, but it looks nice on the shoulder! For a lot of people, this change was extremely important and was fundamental. For a lot of other people, while the change was seen as significant because it publicly hints at changes to policing, it certainly is not fundamental. Indeed, if this was the only change, it would be seen to be merely cosmetic. I hold the view that if you don't follow this sort of symbolic change through with fundamental, substantive change, then it will be just that - cosmetic.

I want to explain to you the other bodies that we have within the Department for Safety and Security. As part of the transformation of policing, a brilliant structure was set up called the Secretariat. But there is an interesting irony of this body. It was called into existence by the new Police Act which makes provision for the establishment of a civilian secretariat whose key responsibility was to provide civilian oversight for the police, in order to monitor the police and also to facilitate transformation. Then, because it was prescribed in the Act, the police took on the responsibility to call the secretariat into existence. So, the police established it, defined its role on the basis of how they understood it, and not how it was meant to be understood, and, to some extent, also influenced the appointment of people in the secretariat - the very structure supposed to provide civilian oversight of the transformation of policing. But if that wasn't enough, in fact the police control the budget, so the secretary of the secretariat is on the pay-roll of the police. So that is a very interesting irony - I should just call it that - though I think probably "contradiction" is more apt. It is certainly an indication of how difficult the task of transformation could be.

So, we had that civilian oversight structure, and in addition the first constitution made provision for the establishment of community police forums. It was written into the functions of the police that every station commission shall establish a community police forum in every police precinct. So, every station commission went out and formed a community police forum - whether it was one, two or three people, whoever it was, getting people off the street to form a community police forum. That was going to happen because the instruction was that it was to be done, so it was done. I want to talk about the implications of regulating bodies into existence as opposed to allowing them to develop organically. Also, we need to look at the relationship between communities and police when structures are imposed upon them.

When I first came into the police they had a Change Management Team and in consultation with some of our Belgian colleagues, we developed a process of changing the police. I don't want to say transformation because I think that has a totally different meaning. We identified all the issues that we had to address to change the police service. We looked, for example, at structures, strategies, resources etc. You have to bear in mind that the SA police was a home for a lot of people. It provided everything from holiday resorts to land, houses, property, everything except a graveyard. You could find everything in the police service. So if you tried to change a police service where you could have - a UK term – 'value for money', it would require identifying the core functions and doing away with the add-ons that do not impact upon your policing functions. You would also ensure that you used the savings to facilitate transformation. That was the idea we had, but because lives of people are affected in such a fundamental way, we had to backtrack on a lot of those change issues. Many people saw policing as their home and they didn't see any alternative other than the police providing for them.

We then went on to identify forty issues that needed changing and needed changing at the same time. Now you must bear in mind that was mid 1994, soon after the elections, and we were so naive. We wanted to change the police and change everything, and do it all at once. There was a pressing need to deliver for the communities. So, we took on what we now call the shotgun approach - we just tried to do everything, of course with very little impact. We have now moved from there to identify key transformation issues one of which is the constitutional requirement to have a police service, and indeed a public service, which is representative of the community it serves. Affirmative action is a key transformation issue. We also need to look at service delivery - not only the nature and the quality of service delivery but also one which is equitable. Here again I should draw your attention to the fact that prior to the elections, seventy four per cent of the police stations were in white areas and business areas, and those which were in black areas were under-resourced. Ill-equipped officers were incapable of delivering anything near or vaguely resembling a police service to the community. So we had those major disparities. Then we also needed to bring about a professional workforce, and we are still grappling with what this concept means. But I think if one keeps it at servicing and equality, equitable service delivery, and one which is representative, then we are moving towards what one wants for a professional workforce. These basically would be our points of emphases.

I should also say to you that one of the key areas we identified among the forty areas was demilitarisation. Now, you would probably ask why wouldn't that be one of our key focus areas? Since the police were known to be a kind of a military police force why isn't that key to transformation? The reason for this is that we attempted demilitarisation when we were trying to do everything all at once. When we changed the uniforms, for example, we did a survey of our members and they were insistent that they didn't want to have a police-cap. The question was - what was the significance of the police cap? After all, in summer in SA it is very hot, but if you see the hat as some sort of protection, then you might want to keep it. So we thought we should retain the police hat in the form of baseball caps. We then realised that the problem was that if officers wore a cap, they had to be saluted and it was because people objected to saluting that the survey highlighted the need for doing away with the cap. So, for a period in 1995,when the service was rationalised, we did away with the police cap and it was no longer essential to wear it. However, police management soon found that when you took away the police cap, and officials were no longer saluting, there was no discipline. Furthermore, if officials were no longer marching straight, or even worse, have given up the practice of marching completely, then there is no discipline at all. This meant that the major discussion at every meeting revolved around the lack of police discipline.   There was a suggestion that the lack of discipline (which was down to human rights!) meant they couldn't do their job properly.

Those arguing for more discipline clearly blamed what they saw as extremely militant police unions for instigating, not only that we have a civilian police, but that we have a totally ill-disciplined police force, who have forgotten what it is to do proper policing - the way it was done twenty years ago etc. So, we had to backtrack a bit on demilitarisation.

My personal feeling is that you should not compromise on demilitarisation - there is no way in a democracy that you could perpetuate a militarised police force. You can't do that - it's one of the non-negotiable items. However, it is how you demilitarise which is extremely important. I would say if you change the symbols, remove the ranks, and change to civilian ranks, that should be the start of the process. However, fundamental to such changes would be a change in the orientation of the police. I quite like the fact that Phil Scraton mentioned this issue of ideology. I think that the language of change has become too glib, too fashionable. It has become too sexy to be talking about things like a police force which is accountable and therefore has to report and seek consent. Police forces have not only to seek consent but to consult with the community about every little thing, sometimes as an excuse, I should say, for not doing actual policing.

So these are the things that were taken on because it was expected of the politicians to do that, when in fact that wasn't the case at all. I think when you talk about demilitarisation you have to look at what needs to change in order to meet the core objectives. So if, for example, you take away military parades, you can take away the military bands, you can take away the military uniform, but if the mind-set is still the same, then you haven't demilitarised. I would rather we keep people in marching formation, that we keep people saluting, but we look at the way we treat people. That should be our starting point and we need also to show the same respect for communities, and then gradually start taking on those things which are the vestiges of a highly militarised police force. I say that because if you ask anyone, they will tell you that the most difficult thing and the most fundamental change besides the insignia was that we have demilitarised. However, the attitude is exactly the same, militarisation is in the mind.

Another point that we have also found very difficult to deal with in the transforming of attitudes is the fact that we have got a police force with about seventy per cent black people. The majority of black people are located in the lower ranks, and as recently as ten years ago, perhaps, black policemen irrespective of their rank, were expected to stand up and salute a white officer, irrespective of his rank. So if you had a case where a white member was a sergeant and the black person was a captain, the black person had to get up and salute the white person first. That has changed but it still takes place in the mind. You have black people who are still so complacent, so passive and so apathetic because of that relationship. It seems that militarisation or even more the power imbalance that existed within the relationship is still there. All of those things impact very strongly on the ability and the capacity of the police to transform itself.

Now that is a question I want to pause on, and I think it is quite key to organisations going through change. The question is whether or not they have the necessary confidence. If you give people a number of guidelines and principles, and they have a legislative framework, is that enough to give us the confidence that police agencies can change? The police has such a strong history, and such a specific occupational culture and mentality. Furthermore, in our case at least, it is an institution that has been under siege and had a very closed culture – 'us and them' - on the attack all the time with an extremely chauvinistic macho culture. Even with a legal framework, is that enough to assume that the police have the capacity and the competency to transform themselves? I would argue that they do not.

The problem here is that, no matter how good the intentions, no matter how much people grab onto and hold onto and read up on things and discuss with people, there are serious limitations because of the culture that has existed over the years. This culture has been institutionalised within individuals. At the same time there is the heightened expectation within communities. You can only manage this tension effectively if you have strong civil society structures impacting directly on the culture of the police. How do you do that, and do you do that from outside, or do you do it from within?

We have a structure called the secretariat which is outside the police - it has its budget, it has its staff, but it has played a very insignificant role in transforming the police. I would say that the extent to which we have transformed the police has largely depended on people coming from outside of the police who were placed and appointed inside the police and who brought about great culture change in the organisation. Why is that? I think it is natural if you grow up in a culture where debate and constructive criticism is part of the make-up of the organisation, and you take that along with you into the police, you start facilitating processes. It is not routine in police institutions for people to constructively challenge their seniors. It is not routine to raise issues within and across the ranks or to take forward discussions and come up with solutions. It's just totally outside the culture and I know many occasions when people came to me and said 'Zelda, you can do it because you are not one of us, you can do it because your advantage is you didn't grow up in the police organisation'. This means that you take on a greater responsibility than others. You can see your advantages and the limitations that other people have; I am saying that there should definitely be more of us in the police to increase the rate of change in the organisation.

So I would want to say that 'our situation is the result of a compromise, and it is the result of a politically negotiated settlement'.   This in itself brought about some limitations but also had some important advantages. For example, if people had had their own way prior to 1994 and we could just have wished away the South African police, then we would have done that without blinking an eye. The organisation was seen to be so notorious, so inherently corrupt and bad, and so disreputable in the eyes of the community, that people would have wanted to wish it away. I would say very confidently that this view would have been the view of the majority of black and oppressed people in South Africa. Our reality, however, determined otherwise. Our reality determined that you had a police force of about 140,000 people, and you had other non statutory bodies, and we had to make do in the best way we possibly could with those resources.

You will have to look at, and we are still having to look at, very creative strategies to fast-track the pace of change because the culture is so pervasive in the organisation, so all pervasive, that if the new intake is small in number, the possibility of being assimilated is extremely great. Before you know it, you cannot tell the difference between "old" and "new". One takes it on lock, stock and barrel for one's own survival and we become like them. However, I think it is very important that we remain true to our conscience. I should say for myself it has been an extremely important learning experience and there are days when I wake up and wonder what am I doing in the police service. But, I would argue that it is a matter of conscience. You often wonder is this the organisation that I want to associate with? But if you look at the broader objective of transforming society for the greater good and you look at the opportunities of developing a democracy, then I have to say to myself that it is all the more worthwhile. I think it is all the more worthwhile because the police and policing structures are crucial safeguards for a developing and lasting peace.

Concluding remarks and summing up

Mary Holland (journalist)

I would also like of course to thank the CAJ. I think it is an extraordinary time for this conference. We meet just after the publication of the Lawrence Inquiry and before Chris Patten's review on the future of the RUC is due to report. But I also think that it is important that the debate should be as broad as possible and hopefully as popular as possible because it is far too important, as Maurice Hayes said in his presentation, to be conducted behind closed doors. I was thinking of how best to draw together some of the threads of discussions and the debates - they have raised some very big questions. How do you, for example, achieve a police force which has the consent and support of both communities? But also some very nitty gritty questions - such as community liaison structures, affirmative action and so forth. I am a journalist, and I thought therefore I would just try to remind you of some of the key quotes or key stories which we have heard in the course of this conference.

I would like first to quote first something that Maurice Hayes (of the Policing Commission) said. He said "we sometimes felt that we were a surrogate Truth and Reconciliation Commission. People told us harrowing stories which highlighted the problem we face as a society in moving beyond the past and into the future". I think that perhaps we have not addressed enough here the legacy of grief and suffering of the victims, and the victims' families. This of course cuts across both communities, - or indeed all the communities I suppose you must say in this forum - but is certainly not the preserve of any particular group. If this issue is not dealt with sensitively, it will explode in our faces. I was very struck by what Zelda said about the emotions being there in the South African police force, and how scary they were because people felt they had to hide them. I assume that what she means is that at some stage those emotions will come out, will indeed burst out, and will come to haunt us. I think that that is a problem which we have to deal with and cannot afford to ignore - because, as I said, it cuts across both communities.

I am sometimes asked what I remember most vividly, and people always think my answer will be the Good Friday Agreement, or when the ceasefire was declared. But in fact what I remember, what I actually carry in my mind, are the images of women and children behind funerals - quite, quite clearly. Once the women and children are following behind the coffins, it does not really matter whether they are the children of an RUC man, or the children of a Catholic who has been killed by the RUC on the Falls Road. The legacy of the grief and the bitterness which will haunt future generations is there regardless.

The second quote I would like to take came from Ralph Crawshaw. I thought he gave us an absolutely inspiring talk about his work with police forces across the world, and trying to put human rights, or a consciousness of human rights, or respect for human rights, right at the centre of policing. Then right at the very end, he said almost as a throwaway remark, "you are taught what to do properly but of course within hours of setting foot on the beat you are told it is all nonsense". That problem of translating the ideal policies and the training which is given to police increasingly in all countries - but certainly in both Britain and Ireland - is how do we translate the theory into practical policing at street level? That problem is something that came up again and again.

Lee Jasper talked about it. How many millions of pounds did the Met spend on race relations, racial sensitivity training, and racial awareness, and yet black people are six to eight times more likely to be picked up in London or stopped in London than white youths are? We struggled, and I am sure all of you did in the workshops, with how that can be changed. Will it be by changing the proportions of Catholics in the RUC by affirmative action, by quotas, or will it be through training? Will it be through making a difference through changing society more generally? Will it be by bringing the police onto liaison committees or bringing them into the community - as someone suggested - inviting them in so that they can become more aware of sensitivities at that level. It was also borne out by a wonderful story that someone from the Ardoyne told us. She said, either in our workshop or in one of the plenary sessions, "I have been on delegations to the RUC police stations and to RUC headquarters and I have been treated with the utmost courtesy, given tea and biscuits and treated like a lady. Then I go down onto the streets and I am immediately addressed as a 'Fenian slut'". A lot of the discussion in our workshop focussed on these problems.

I also liked very much Zelda Holtzman's story of the saga of whether or not the new South African police force or the new South African recruits should be forced to wear a cap. You abolish the idea of a cap and saluting because you want to have more equality and presumably a greater sense of camaraderie - you want to encourage more egalitarianism within the force - but you find discipline is going to hell. And, of course, for many, discipline is seen as absolutely necessary because a large part of the function of policing is to impose and to secure safety and security for the community as a whole. That very often involves taking action which is seen as strict and punitive.

I am keeping this brief because I know there will be many comments from the floor, and I am very, very conscious that I have not talked much about structures and training, and those debates in the workshops, and in the plenary sessions. But finally I think that for someone like myself, perhaps the most important thing is to look at the underlying theme of this conference – the huge task we all face of achieving a police force which commands the support of the whole community.

The RUC, for better or worse, is reflective of our society. I believe, the institution is a symptom of the problems that face that society, and of its bitter divisions. The whole emphasis of the conference really has been on the need to change, but it also needs to be said that there is a very, very large section of the community in Northern Ireland that sees the police as the heroes of the last thirty years, the victims of the last thirty years. The police have suffered very greatly, and these people do not see any need for change. Indeed they regard change, the ideas of change that are being canvassed, let alone the calls for abolition or disbandment, as an attack on their community. These people also need to be convinced that change is necessary. They need to be made to believe that change will benefit them, as well as the nationalist community which has traditionally been at the receiving end of the RUC's activities.

So, I think it is a necessary and important question, an absolutely necessary question to ask, as Sir William MacPherson asked of the Metropolitan police - is the RUC riddled with institutionalised sectarianism? I think, however, it is also important to realise that if it is, it reflects the sectarianism rife in society as a whole. We all have to look into our own hearts to see how that can be eradicated - we cannot expect to leave it to the police alone. Thank you.

Bea Campbell (journalist)

Like Mary Holland, I feel that this event has been one of those memorable, transforming, episodes in one's life, when one is part of a number of different conversations happening all at the same time. At one level perhaps, the Policing Commission itself should take comfort from and be reassured by this experience. We have all got very different dispositions, and yet we have sat for two days with each other talking about what is felt to be the most dangerous theme in Northern Ireland society – the administration of policing! Despite this, we are all alive, and we will all go out of the room still alive having survived the conversation! I think myself that is a clue to how policing in all societies is perceived. It is a kind of radioactive theme. Yet, at the same time, it is like illness in hospitals - we all want to have our say, and we are all experts in that conversation. And, generally speaking human beings, being what they are, do manage to have these kind of conversations, and live to fight another day!

I say that because something ran through this last couple of days - Mary alluded to it as well - that is very important, yet very difficult for the Policing Commission to hold onto. I learned it in the course of some of our workshops, where we had a very specific agenda to address: accountability and operational autonomy is the one that sticks in my mind. It was very difficult for our workshop to get a grip of that conversation, because there was something that came before that conversation. Even if we had known how to discuss it and I don't think we did, the thing that preceded that conversation was all about hurt, and harm, and humiliation. That reminded me of the first public meeting, I believe, that the Policing Commission had in, I think, West Belfast. A huge public meeting, comprised of hundreds of people turning out to have their conversation about policing and peace, with representatives of the Commission who had come into their community to listen to them. What, of course, they gave to the Policing Commission, was a litany of grief. Very politely, about two thirds of the way through that meeting - I expect you remember it if you were there - the chair of the Policing Commission said politely, "Thank you for telling us about your experiences, and if more of you want to tell us about your experiences, fine - but we would also be very interested in positive suggestions about future arrangements." Now, I have no doubt that the Policing Commission learned instantly that it had made a mistake in saying that.

First of all because everything that was said about what people felt about their personal biography, and their community biography, was of course very positive. They were able to speak in public in a room to each other and to people they didn't know - a very risky thing to do.   Moreover, those experiences defined what they might be interested in and enabled them to think about what the shape of a policing service might look like, or might need to look like, in the future. It wasn't unruly, it was extraordinarily disciplined. Usually, in my experience, people - when they get the chance to speak - are very disciplined about how they enunciate their feelings. What also was revealed is that you cannot have one single kind of conversation about the structural, administrative and managerial arrangements of a major public service that touches directly upon points of conflict and oppression in a society. You need to allow a lot of the conversations to take place about what that oppression and conflict felt like.

What is also important is that the whole conversation in Northern Ireland about policing coincides with the "trans-island" conversation about policing. Indeed, it is a global conversation about policing. We have reached a point where all societies are having to contemplate whether the model of policing based largely on the British template works in complex modern societies. Does it work to have that model of law-enforcement as a major public presence, as one of the great - if you like - edifices, of every society's sense of itself? Does it makes sense to have that traditional template of policing when we now understand that there are a proliferation of points of conflict, points of oppression, points of disorder, points of law-breaking?   The old-fashioned notion that all you had to do in order to be a police service was to enforce the law has changed in the last thirty years.

What I am trying to suggest to you is that in the last thirty years there has been a transformation in our sense of what constitutes the points of power, oppression, conflict, rights and responsibilities in our society, and also a proliferation in our sense of where violence and oppression, law-breaking etc arise. So, what we should take confidence from, and what I am suggesting, is that the terms of the entire global conversation about policing is in contention. Everywhere people are involved in the vexed, difficult argument about what would a future, sensible, efficient, police service look like, and nobody has the answer. The particular difficulty in Northern Ireland is that the conversation is also influenced by another very different conversation about the nature of the historic political settlement here.

One of the things that I think again we should take heart from is the nature of the Agreement in Northern Ireland. Parallels can be drawn with the Lawrence Inquiry, and certainly the Lawrence Inquiry saw itself as a signal moment. It gave Britain permission to talk about policing, not just in terms of the black experience of policing - which is pretty awful and universally awful probably. But also the Inquiry allowed and gave us all permission to look at the detail of the work of policing. The saga that emerges in the context of the Lawrence Inquiry is that that extraordinary, devastating, apparently eternal, inefficiency is not exceptional but in fact typical of the difficulties that many communities experience in getting access to a decent policing service. The people who are most disappointed in policing, as it happened, are not just people like the Lawrence family - but any old family in any old place. It was very, very difficult for them to get the service to which they are entitled and, as it happens, very difficult for the police to deliver the service which those people think they are entitled to, and that many people within the police community wish they could deliver. That conversation has been going on for a long time within the police community itself. It is one of the more useful things that periodically happens. Police officers talk about their own feelings, about the difficulty of delivering a service which is not very good, living within a professional community that is not very good, bolstering itself and defending itself against that everyday reality of disappointment and inefficiency by highly militaristic and highly hierarchical internal structures. But these structures in turn make it very difficult for the police to have an ordinary conversation with themselves, still less with those outside the institution.

I remember vividly the words of a police commander in the city in which I live (which is Newcastle upon Tyne) where there was a riot in 1991. This man commanded the police operation that intervened in this riot situation, and he is haunted by a tape-recording that he keeps in his desk. The tape-recording is of Asian residents of a housing estate who escaped the estate within inches of their lives. He plays that tape to himself periodically because he knows that it was only by the grace of God that there were no dead people. We are talking about Newcastle upon Tyne - not Belfast. But he had an experience that I imagine many people serving in the RUC here have also experienced - the chill of having that tape, or a mental tape, that reminds you of what you did or did not manage to do, to enable people to feel safe in the place they live. I know that the Newcastle police officer plays the tape endlessly to himself.

All of the people who felt unsafe and who could no longer live in that estate were black. The riot was never described as a "race riot" because those rioting were white. This tells you something very important about the confusion we have in society about what constitutes race and what doesn't constitute race. You know of course, I am not a race - me - since, as you can see, I am white! I have no ethnic history!

I digress, but one of the things I suppose is useful for Northern Ireland's conversation with itself about policing is something that you may feel is actually not relevant at all, which is the Lawrence Inquiry. Partly, as I said earlier, because it gives a very useful description of ordinary police practice. With that inflection of a devastating racial murder, it is illuminating because where it becomes radioactive and dangerous is precisely at that point where racism meets operational inefficiency. That is one of the things I think has been difficult to talk about in this context. This global conversation about policing is happening at a time when the typical composition of the police forces is being actively challenged. Policing is probably unique. What public service is 90% masculinised and 90% white? Well, it might be 90% white, but it certainly wouldn't be 90% masculine. How on earth does anybody think at this point in history that a 90% masculinised service is anything that anybody would want to be served by? The entire history of the most masculinised institution on the planet earth is a disaster with shards of extraordinary ingenuity and creativity. But in its ordinary routine way of going about its business, it is disastrous. In civil society everybody knows this. Nobody would dream of organising a society in that way if they could help it. The trouble is that political society, and policing are probably the only two relics of the old order remaining. They make it very difficult to imagine something different but you have been given permission in Northern Ireland to use your imagination and I wish we in Britain had been given the same permission. There is a prescription in the Agreement about representativity, participation, inclusivity and accountability that gives you the opportunity, I think, to imagine what a police service that isn't made up of 90% white Protestant men would look like. It would look probably like an awful lot of people in this room. It is something that only moments of crisis give you permission to investigate.

My worry is that the Commission, given its terms of reference and its sense of its own imperative, will feel driven to be in a great hurry to come up with administrative answers to political problems. In a sense it may move rather too hastily to look at managerial, structural, and organisational issues. These issues do not comfortably fit with the big difficult question that this society has at last allowed itself to ask. This brings me to the final point I wish to make - which is to do with the relationship between grief and the creation of a new order.

I suppose that, at least in the short term encompassed by the recent '90s, one of South Africa's greatest gifts to the planet has been the Truth and Reconciliation Commission. It has had an amazing story to tell to the country itself and to the rest of the world. I am minded of the testimony of a man involved in the Truth Commission who was asked a question about forgiveness. That question haunts me as I think about the Policing Commission meetings - those thirty odd meetings that have been organised around Northern Ireland. The meetings were held often in places where people from completely polarised experiences managed to be in the same room as each other. This was a very hard thing to do, and indeed a very brave thing probably for most of them to do. But what was very striking about it, about those meetings was the extraordinary discipline that the protagonists in those meetings brought to the business of bearing witness to their own history and giving their experience to the Policing Commission. The second thing that was very telling about those experiences was how difficult it is to translate one's personal experience into an administrative or structural template.

There was perhaps a natural rush to move from that dangerous business of emotion and feeling into practical arrangements. The latter were often offered as alternatives, and there was an insistent demand that contributors help come up with an administrative template that would solve the problem. Maybe something different has to happen; maybe those two things cannot happen without each other. The South African experience tells us that it is a terrifying process to put yourself through, but also if you do not do it, you do not know who you are. If you do not know what you are, you do not know what you need to do. It is a bit like living in a society where you don't have any statistics about suicide. What do you know about your society, if you do not know why people kill themselves?

But, to return to the South African man's experience. He was asked whether, having given his testimony, he was prepared to forgive the officers who killed his wife. He said "No, but I can share my country with them". That was telling us something again terribly important – that people are extraordinarily resilient. However, if they are not given permission to tell their story, then they are not being given permission to be themselves.   They are not being given permission to participate in the process of change and of transformation. I am mindful of what Zelda Holtzman said about the different terms now used to describe a police service in South Africa - one that is less concerned with "law enforcement" and more concerned with what it means to be "safe" and to be "secure". Maybe these are things that we can appropriate within our own conversation.

But just like the global conversation about the organisation of police that is happening, a second global conversation which resonates very much with the conversation in Northern Ireland is taking place. Thus, the twentieth century is a century in which people bear witness in an entirely new way. And one of the things that is at stake in the process of bearing witness is the extraordinary difficulty of conveying, particularly when your very person has been abused, is a very real sense of how your own physical and emotional integrity has been assaulted. Telling your story is both one of the most difficult things that you could do and one of the most vital things for you to do, and we mustn't underestimate how vital it is. The second thing of course is that testimony, or bearing witness, demands something else very, very difficult, and that is the hazard of listening. After all, you put your own experience at risk if you allow your experience to assimilate with the experience of someone else.

What I am suggesting finally is that what we seem to have learned from the series of events that the CAJ has organised, and the series of meetings that the Policing Commission has organised, is that people's determination to tell their story about how they have lived for the last thirty years will not stop. Indeed, it should not stop. Therefore, some accommodation has to be found for that conversation. If it's true that the Policing Commission is not a Truth and Reconciliation Commission, maybe one of the things it could suggest is that what Northern Ireland needs is a Truth and Reconciliation Commission? At the same time, its task as a Policing Commission can be serviced by and guided by the experience of truth and reconciliation. Finally, in order to service the conversation about the creation of a new kind of order and a new kind of public peace in Northern Ireland, maybe the Policing Commission needs to re-think its approach. It should perhaps not expect that the people of Northern Ireland tell the Commission straightforwardly what needs to be done, and that they come up spontaneously with good and positive ideas about future policing. Instead, or alongside the listening process, there should be some attempt at servicing the conversation, so that people know what some of the various alternatives are, and what some of the various models are. The CAJ has done some of this pro-active support work with nil resources; maybe the Policing Commission should also do it, given its more considerable resources?

I do not believe that people can have a useful conversation about a future police service unless they are resourced to have it, and unless they feel that their issues about grief, pain and pride are also given a hearing.

Vote of thanks

Peter Smith, QC
member of the Policing Commission

Ladies and Gentlemen,

I would like to express, on behalf of the Independent Commission, our gratitude for the time and trouble that everyone who has been here yesterday and today has taken to make such an invaluable contribution to our work, and I will illustrate in a moment what I really mean by that. The many ideas that have arisen over the last few days will be carried back by the members of the secretariat, and in particular by Maurice Hayes and myself who are members of the Commission, and they will be discussed in detail in due course. May I also express our gratitude to the eminent speakers who have contributed to the debate by sharing their particular experiences and expertise with us.

One of the striking things, and of course many things have stimulated ideas as I have listened to the speakers, but one of the most interesting is that, despite the fact that the background of practically all of the speakers has been quite different, the similarity of their experiences has been really very marked indeed. It is striking that the problems of policing are universal. Many of the problems that we are aware of in Northern Ireland are echoed, perhaps in slightly different or markedly different forms, but echoed nevertheless in countries right across the world. That, on the one hand, is disconcerting but on the other hand reassuring, because it means that a very large number of people are working on the very same problems that we are facing.

May I also mention that I found the workshop yesterday very interesting and very useful. Whenever I read the allocation of workshop rooms, I naturally assumed that I would be regarded as an "orange sticker"[20] but I was flattered,

---

[20] This is an allusion to the fact that all conference participants were pre-assigned to workshops which simultaneously debated the same topics. The pre-allocation was intended to ensure that in each workshop there would be a broad spread of expertise. The colour coding for the workshops - as indicated - had no significance!

as I rather like the appellation, to find that I in fact was a "black asterisk". I would like to pay a special tribute to the other "black asterisks" who shared several hours yesterday with me.

I said earlier that I would explain how particularly valuable the last few days have been and I make particular reference to the workshop. I said very little in the workshop yesterday, because it seemed to me that the important thing was to listen to the other members of the workshop and hear what they had to say. Bea (Campbell) earlier mentioned our public meeting in the Whiterock Education Centre in West Belfast, and she is absolutely right in saying that we quickly detected at that meeting our naivete. We had had the naive idea that we would have a series of public meetings, people would make presentations to us, and then we would engage in a dialogue with them. But, it quickly became apparent that that was never going to happen. It just does not happen like that in West Belfast. We also had the experience of going to Coleraine - which is where I come from. I had predicted, from my immense knowledge of Northern Ireland, and my knowledge indeed of the Coleraine area, that we would have a poorly attended meeting, that petered out after an hour and twenty minutes, and everybody would go home early. Of course, we had hundreds of people who spoke with the same passion, as it were, from the other side of the great divide, and with exactly the same depth of feeling as we had listened to and heard in the experience in West Belfast.

I just want to make it absolutely clear that even though the way the meetings worked out turned out to be very different from my expectation, they nevertheless in their own way were extremely valuable, and I have to express our gratitude to the people who attended. It was not easy for them, in front of several hundred people, to stand up and to divulge the appalling experiences that so many people on both sides of the community have experienced over the last thirty years. However, because of the absence of dialogue, it meant that we were left having listened to these experiences without being able to engage in discussion. As was mentioned, the chairman posed the dilemma - 'we hear the pain but where do we go from here?'. That is where this kind of conference has been extremely valuable.

Even though I myself did not engage in the workshop debate, many of the questions that came into my mind as I have listened to the speakers and listened in the workshop were actually taken up by other participants in the workshop, so that my questions were answered in a way that was actually more spontaneous and in a way that I myself could not have expected them to be answered if I had taken the lead. So I do want to express appreciation not only to the speakers at these plenary sessions, but also I would like to express appreciation for the value of the workshops.

May I conclude by thanking the CAJ, and the many members of the CAJ, who have contributed to the organisation that went before and to the superb organisation of the last two days. Frankly, if it wasn't for your organisation, our task would be immensely more difficult, and whatever problems we are going to face in terms of coming to our conclusions, that task will have been greatly facilitated by your organisation. I refer not just (invaluable as it has been) to this conference over the last couple of days, but also your involvement and engagement with us in the past since we began our task, which I hope very much will continue in whatever form that it is mutually advantageous between now and the summer of 1999 when we report. In thanking you, thanking you all, and thanking the CAJ in particular and the distinguished speakers, may I express the hope that you all enjoy the rest of your weekend.

Workshop Reports

Morning sessions: Composition and Training

Workshop A

There was firstly a discussion of **training and education** and there was a sense that one needed some overall vision. On the one hand, there was a need to focus on who should be recruited/retained and promoted within policing, but there was also a need to determine who the police should serve and be seen to serve?

As to the people needed within policing there was a feeling that staff - and the overall institution - needed to be principled, disciplined, accountable, non-militaristic, inclusive, representative and objective.

Interestingly, the issue of who does the police serve, can be and has been more difficult - are they there to serve the community, to uphold the law, to defend the state, or to protect human rights. There was some feeling that the concept of protecting human rights might in practice prove to be a unifying theme since if it were taken as the guiding principle it would ensure that the police did all the other things expected of them (upholding the law, serving the community and defending the state, at least to the extent that the state represents the whole of society).

In this context, there was some suggestion that some of the current policing budget should be "diverted" into more community based initiatives. Such a trend would also be useful to the extent that it begins to fudge the current very sharp dichotomy between what is thought to be "community policing" on the one hand and "state policing" on the other.

As to the issue of **composition** in terms of practical suggestions, there were a number of specific proposals. For example,

- clear person and job specifications are needed for recruiting to the police;
- there is a need for more effective monitoring, of an internal and external nature;

- merit should be retained as the guiding principle, but perhaps it should be understood to include the merit to be achieved by developing a police service with all the diverse skills and experience needed in policing
- effective outreach measures: is research being done currently on where police adverts are being placed, who is coming forward, who is not coming forward, what in the present culture or structures is attracting certain kinds of people and not others?

Pre-recruitment is also important in this context. Recruits should show some evidence of their competence, or their ability to develop a competence, in the key skills required - especially the ability to exercise discretion without abusing powers.

As to *training* - it was thought important to get across the right cultural messages in training:
- conciliation skills
- a holistic approach to training
- community awareness
- the need to take people seriously
- human rights
- ethos of efficiency

and that some of these skills could be imparted in community colleges etc.

There needs to be an openness around training and this will be essential both to open the police up to external civilian influences, and to educate communities about how to inter-act effectively and develop relationships of trust.

There was a sense that the design of training is very important. Who is currently involved in consultations around training design? Who owns the process? How do we ensure life-long learning? Should we not ensure training and education in different experiential situations such as community colleges etc.

Human rights cannot be an "add-on" to the training process but must be a fully integrated part of it. There has to be effective monitoring if we are to ensure that the proposed changes translate into real change on the ground.

Workshop B

Several commentators spoke about the good experience that can be easily drawn upon from elsewhere - the real problem is in turning international good practice into practice at street level and within management structures and practices.

An important change in the situation at present is that, in the wake of the Agreement and the Northern Ireland Act, all public bodies have to carry out equality impact assessments and the police will presumably be obliged to do this also. Of course the RUC is currently subject to sex discrimination legislation and there are relatively few women in the force, so one must wonder if the change will be that obvious. However, the statutory duty will extend protection to the broader equality front and the very fact that the public sector generally will be expected not merely not to discriminate, but to actively promote equality of opportunity, could prove very valuable.

But there was anyway some uncertainty about how one deals with racism, sexism, sectarianism etc. in the force. Can these 'isms be "trained out" of the force. The Lawrence Inquiry would seem to suggest not, and there is no point in spending millions of pounds on race relations training if this has little or no impact on endemic racism. There was some discussion of a specific intensive training project currently underway with a small number of officers selected from across a number of ranks. The work of Mediation Network in this regard is seen very positively by the RUC, and these kinds of intensive initiatives complement the broader community awareness programme that all officers (including the Chief Constable) should be required to undertake.

In response to questions about the relationship between police and the Catholic community, people were referred to the community awareness programme (which introduces all officers to an understanding of different communities, including the Catholic one) and to the rapid response times that police maintain in response to all call-outs. The latter statistics were proffered to counter the common perception in many Catholic areas that the police do not respond effectively to call-outs - the answer suggested that the police made no distinction between different localities.

Drawing on English policing experiences, one contributor spoke of the practice of senior police officers - subsequent to Scarman - of using the "right" language but not necessarily being able or willing to deal with the "hard" issues. What is really needed is to engage with issues of power. Thus, when we discuss training and composition, we cannot focus on individuals and their behaviour, but we need to consider the police as an institution operating within a political context and as exercising extensive powers.

This accorded with the view of those who felt that the "rotten apple" theory was too simplistic and too convenient. The Met has got to come to grips with the issue of institutional racism in the wake of the MacPherson report and this has to, and can only, be tackled at the political and policy making level. Indeed, the point was made that training can often be an excuse not to tackle these bigger questions. By revamping training, senior officers may feel that they have done enough and can point to new or improved training programmes as "the solution". In its turn, there is then the risk that people claim that something (human rights abuses, sectarianism, racism etc.) cannot be happening, because the training programme has rooted out all such tendencies. Just as human rights cannot be an "add on" to training, training cannot be an "add on" to policing policy.

Indeed, police training has also to take into account society's attitudes and the problems this creates in its new recruits. New recruits when thinking of the Chinese, think take-away shops and triads! The Lawrence Inquiry is highlighting that we need to start changing such stereotypes in the school curriculum.

But, the key questions still remain for policing in Northern Ireland - what do we want the composition of the police to be, how do we avoid charges of either direct or indirect discrimination in creating a more pluralist force, and what pro-active recruitment measures are acceptable and effective? The example was given that the Employment Equality Review proposed (and the government later agreed) that employers could actively recruit from amongst the long term unemployed, even though this would disproportionately benefit Catholics.

What techniques would be appropriate in our attempts to make policing more representative?

It was noted that the public meetings of the Policing Commission had by and large shared a consensus around the need for the police to be representative. But how would this work? For ethnic minorities, for example, there was a sense that institutional racism will have to be tackled before anyone would apply to the police; the early ethnic minority recruits cannot be used as a political football or suffer racist harassment at the hands of their colleagues. There needs to be a parallel process whereby confidence in the community is gradually developed. Indeed we are talking of a two-way process whereby communities and the police need to engage constructively and build up trust in both directions.

This of course however raises the dilemma for many people of how do communities engage when they are totally alienated from the police and have no desire to engage with a discredited organisation. Many see disbandment as the only way forward - the only way which would allow us to leave aside the legacy of the past and allow for a building of trust and dialogue. But, at the same time, there are others within the community who fear the push for disbandment and, in many instances, see this as arising solely from a different political perspective, rather than having anything to do with differential policing experiences. Maybe the way forward is to determine what kind of policing we would all want to see, and this vision would allow us to determine whether it was the kind of institution one wanted to join.

Clearly this dilemma of securing community support for policing was much more than what was understood by the term "community policing".

Brainstorming about these new policing arrangements, people thought that methodologies would have to change, guns would need to go, attitudes to Travellers would need to change, in-depth community consultation would be a pre-requisite... But there is still the problem of the political context within which the police operate. If one looks at developments in public order policing generally (not just in NI), policing has become more a matter of police discretion than ever, and the responses have become more draconian than ever. These trends reflect decisions being made at the macro political level where patriarchy and class attitudes predominate and infuse structures and institutional responses. It is these broader structural issues which need to be addressed if one is to exercise effective power over policing.

In Northern Ireland, a concrete example of this is the all-pervasive emergency power construct within which policing has always been done. Emergency powers undermine good policing, and there is little point in talking of community relations training, mechanisms for accountability, changing the composition of the force, as long as such powers are retained. For, as long as they are retained, a macho, militaristic, human rights abusive culture, is the relatively natural institutional product.

Moreover, it is difficult to imagine how the force can shrug off this past. Will nationalists ever accept the RUC, regardless of the changes brought about and regardless of how much work is done to change the composition? The history of the past made the force pre-eminently political and calls for change from the UN or whoever have been almost consistently ignored. Some believe that there is no way that an RUC officer who has policed a conflict situation can turn into a police officer operating in "normal" circumstances. The only acceptable option for many nationalists will be that we start afresh with a blank page, although some agree that former officers can be allowed to re-apply.

Other contributors noted that there was a huge policing vacuum in areas like the Shankill too and though there was no call for disbandment in unionist areas, there was often a call for "huge reform".

But the disband/reform argument, even if it could be answered to everyone's satisfaction, still leaves lots of questions unanswered. After all, while reform means taking the route of changing institutional culture, and the alternative is to change the very institution itself - in either case, the bottom line is surely what are the criteria for determining who can be a police officer?

Moreover, in a situation where we need to bring about a major reduction in the numbers of police - whether we are talking about redundancies from the present force, or building an entirely new one - we have an almost insurmountable problem. We cannot think that change will occur by some kind of "trickle-down" effect. That will just not work, and we are going to have to engage in a whole series of difficult but inter-connecting themes.

Consideration will have to be given to lay-offs, affirmative action measures, a major series of legal reforms, a vetting process etc. Whatever we do, there should not be a random scape-goating of individuals, and we are going to have to develop clear criteria that people wanting to be police officers in future will need to meet.

There was also a sense that the whole difficult issue would be greatly assisted if there were a broader society-wide debate about what happened during the conflict. People need to hear of the different experiences of others if they are to have any understanding of their different demands regarding policing. Indeed police officers who have been hurt and bereaved need also to be allowed to come to terms with their own difficulties as well as those of others.

The big challenge for the Policing Commission is whether we can start new policing arrangements without starting from a completely fresh sheet; and, whatever the answer to that question, how will the necessary political will be generated behind their eventual recommendations for the way forward?

Workshop C

1. A police force should be seen by the community it polices as (a) independent; (b) available to all; (c) dedicated to upholding the rights of individuals within society.

2. To reflect the changes which have taken place in NI, change to the police force is required.

3. Those changes would include: (a) carefully drawn criteria on entry; (b) screening of existing officers; (c) encouragement of a broader cross-section of community, with all groups represented; (d) proper education and training of existing officers; (e) reduction in numbers.

4. There was recognition of the high cost in financial and human terms of these changes and therefore of the need for sensitivity and fairness.

5.   Views differed on the role of quotas: (a) concern was expressed that it was intensely unfair and wrong to use any yardstick other than merit; (b) concern was expressed that tokenism is not enough and change in critical mass would be required.

6.   Views also differed as to the pace of change: (a) some felt realism meant that one was only likely to see real change over a generation or more; (b) others were more impetuous/optimistic; (c) all agreed some changes could and should be made immediately.

Workshop D

There was firstly an exchange around the current symbols and culture of the RUC and the sense in which these alienate some within society. If the police is to be "ours" then it needs to be one where the symbols and culture reflects the diversity that is society. The Canadian example was thought to be a useful one in this regard, and how they have responded to the multi-cultural challenges facing the police.

Some within the group felt that the issue of symbols was more one of perception - so the Falls Road might perceive that the current arrangements exclude them, but this is not necessarily a perception shared on the Shankill. But this led onto a discussion of the differential experiences people have of policing. Whether one is a nationalist or a unionist, a middle class or working class person, a man or a woman, black or white, young or old... policing is often experienced quite differentially. Certainly this is the experience in other jurisdictions, and this experience, as well as the perceptions about these differential experiences, all need to be catered to.

But how do we get from where we are now to something we can all lend credence to in the future? What happens in any interim period? For example, there is much discussion of community policing, but there is a problem as to what constitutes serious crime, and who determines what is/is not serious crime? The restorative justice projects which currently exist have a somewhat awkward relationship with the statutory sector - should the latter be involved from the outset, at a later stage, or only as a back-up to local resources? Can we rely on the new Policing Ombudsman to ensure more effective accountability, and how is this done with greater local level community control? Could a bottom-up approach lead to more fragmentation and less opportunity for clear lines of accountability?

In Catalonia, they had not got rid of all the former police personnel, but the departure of some key people who were seen to have been living in the past was an important impetus to change. People seeing key people leaving saw that things began to change. Of course, a vital issue is what is done with those who are retained or new recruits. It was felt that there needs to be an emphasis on life-long learning and an emphasis on matching the theory with experience and practice. It is natural (but unacceptable) that new recruits go out onto the street and are told to forget all the theory they got during their training. Training must be constantly assessed and re-assessed to ensure that it matches the needs on the ground and that it does equip officers with the skills they need "out on the streets".

Such training however is part of a cyclical process. People (the police and their critics) need to see the need for change and they need to evolve outcomes that are based on sound principles. Such a recognition would increase confidence in NGOs and in the wider public generally and this would in turn lead to good practice development involving police and community. Monitoring and reviews of policing are extremely important.

It was felt that there were important lessons to learn from elsewhere. In many places there was no possibility of disbanding the security forces because the balance of power would not allow it (look, for example, at the situation in Chile). But, elsewhere, there might be a value in looking at attitudes to policing in places like the Republic of Ireland where the Gardai are seen much more as helpers and servants. In Catalonia, there are a number of different issues looked at in the testing process. Firstly, potential recruits are tested against a variety of cultural factors; medical/physical/linguistic factors; and then a series of psychological tests that look at ability to withstand stress, problem solving skills, ability to think laterally etc. There then follows several months of a training regime and at the end of this, recruits are often rejected. The selection process is very rigorous.

At the same time, it was thought that we should not import simplistic solutions from elsewhere. There is no similar sense of "closure" here as in a number of other countries that we might be tempted to look at. But does this mean that the macro political stuff needs to be worked out in order to move ahead at all, or is there an inter-play with the macro and micro levels of conflict resolution?

If we are to change the composition of the police, the practical methods which jump to mind include quotas, ratios, advertising jobs in different languages and different areas, leafleting certain groups and constituencies. How do we recruit people from a nationalist background and give them space to retain and be respected for their political identities and beliefs? There was some discussion of developing a register of political beliefs and organisational membership, but the problem with this is that data gathering of this kind could interfere with a recruit's right to privacy.

Moreover, there are problems which go beyond merely those of dramatically changing the composition. What about issues of inefficiency, the culture of self-protectionism etc. The revelation of the Stephen Lawrence Inquiry in Britain was that there was a lot of brutality and inefficiency in practice within police ranks.

One important way forward is to civilianise the whole operation of policing much more. Lawyers, sociologists, management consultants, all need to be involved. At the community level, there must also be an effort to educate the communities and dispense with punishment methods such as beatings etc. Such activities are deeply offensive and counter-productive and new alternative ways of dealing with anti-social behaviour need to be evolved.

Last but not least, the working group discussed the parameters of a "neutral working environment". There was some challenging of why any flags were needed at all.

Workshop E

The debate centred around a discussion of policing change generally but focusing at certain points on issues of composition and training. A theme that ran through the whole debate was that fundamental changes are required within both the state and society before any specific issues of policing can be addressed. The state was seen as having a number of different influences.

The first of these was that the nature of the state has led to a very conservative ethos within the police force so that certain minority groups eg gays feel particularly apprehensive about approaching the police with any problems they might have. The second point regarding the state was that, occasionally, problems must also be attributed to how certain laws have been introduced or framed by the state rather than attributing all the blame to how they are implemented by the police eg sexual offences laws as well as emergency laws. Thirdly, it was thought that the organs of the state need to be properly implemented and supported before a proper policing system can be enforced. If there isn't community support for the political system, it will be impossible to have an acceptable police force as part of that system.

Another central theme in the discussion was that fundamental change is needed in attitudes within both society and the police before issues of composition and training can effectively be addressed. As regards society, a number of points arose. Firstly, there was the recognition that both the conscious and unconscious sectarianism that presently exist in society serves to hinder any progress that could potentially be made in reforming the police. Until society faces up to certain issues, particularly unconscious sectarianism, the effectiveness of reform will be limited. Linked to this, it was also stressed that human rights education/training needs to begin in the community, people need to recognise that as well as having rights they have the responsibility to extend those rights to others.

As regards attitudes within the RUC, it was felt that these needed to change before more specific problems of composition and training can be tackled. An example of this is the case of young people; obviously changing composition will not directly improve their experiences with the police, only an attitudinal change can do this. A strong view that came across was that as part of this attitudinal change, the RUC will have to become "self-critical"; accept that they have made mistakes and that problems have occurred. It was felt that only after these issues are tackled can progress be made.

This group was reluctant to make proposals or be creative about measures needed to tackle problems with composition and training. The only thoughts offered on training were that it need to be an ongoing process in order to be effective; thus the need to train existing officers as well as new recruits is important. The point raised by the speaker Ralph Crawshaw was also emphasised ie that a lot can be lost in the transition from training to actually being on the street and that measures are needed to address this, but again few constructive suggestions as to how to do this were made. As regards composition, it was recognised that this was a larger issue than simply the two communities, but there were few creative ideas as to how better representation could be achieved.

In conclusion, then, the group felt that it was premature to contemplate issues of composition and training until more fundamental problems relating to attitudes within society and the police were solved.

Afternoon sessions - Accountability

Workshop F

The key points arising from the meeting were as follows:

a.   There was a concern about how one avoids the potential conflict between on the one hand accountability to the local community, and on the other accountability for upholding human rights. Examples considered included the problem of punishment beatings, and the difficulties often posed when a paedophile moves into a local area.

b.   Also what do we mean by the term "community" when talking of policing. Not all communities are based in a specific locality e.g. ethnic minorities, gays and lesbians

c.   Police constables are not "employees" in the ordinary sense. There was a sense that they should be made subject to ordinary employment laws and rules. However, the protection of rights should be written into the job description and human rights violations should be made sackable offences.

d.   There is scope for a statutory monitoring team to be called in if police think that they may need to use force. Police should have to explain their operational decisions to the team which then observes, reports and analyses lessons to be learnt for the future. This would be an extension of the kind of thing CAJ was doing during the parades.

There was a lot of discussion of the RUC's failure to be accountable for "operational" decisions, and the fact that the doctrine of "operational independence" provides de facto impunity for the police from being held to account for their actions.

Workshop G

In a general exchange about the presentations made in the plenary session, some people made the direct analogy between the policing experience of nationalists and what had been happening around the Lawrence Inquiry. Correlations with experiences in loyalist areas were also highlighted.

Cases like the Peter McBride one, and the reinstatement of the two Guardsmen, gave a very negative signal. It suggested that these two officers were fit to serve in the army (and presumably also therefore in the police) when, even if released, they had clearly been found guilty of serious crimes and misdemeanours. The RUC in not recognising its responsibilities vis-à-vis all the communities here cannot hope to be properly accountable.

New accountability arrangements will need to operate at several levels and there certainly cannot be one single body - whether independent or not - which carries all the burden of holding the police to account. A variety of levels and bodies need to hold the police to account, from recruitment stage through to senior management. And what does one do about past failures in accountability? For example, people in leadership positions now in the RUC were performing key managerial functions already at the time of a spate of shoot-to-kill allegations - what does this mean in terms of their role now and in the future, and the same issues apply presumably to many other officers in the current force. We need to develop positive models for the future, but how do we deal with the past, so that people can have confidence in the personnel and the institutions responsible for policing in future?

The Catalonian example was drawn upon to emphasise how important they had found it to create partnerships between the police and community.   In evolving future arrangements, both "sides" needed to be prepared to seek accommodation and compromise somewhat. This led into a discussion about the factors necessary to make an investigation truly independent? the kinds of people necessary to carry out such investigations? the need to be fair to all involved, providing legal advice and support, while at the same time making the process as open and transparent as possible, so that ordinary complainants are not intimidated by the adversarial nature of the process.

There is a real potential conflict between operational independence and accountability and there needs to be a clear definition of the respective authority of the Police Authority and the Chief Constable in relation to operational matters.   Currently the Chief Constable is essentially entirely autonomous. But even once one agrees about the respective functions of the Police Authority and the Chief Constable, there is a need to clarify who the Police Authority is responsible to?

A discussion ensued around the policy of plastic bullets as an exemplar of the problem around accountability. It is difficult to ascertain who gives the go-ahead for the deployment of plastic bullets. In the US the elected officials - in the shape of the local mayor or governor - can step in and take control of policing issues. The risk with this model of course is that it can lead to too much political interference. We need somehow to civilianise the accountability process without falling into political partisanship.

People were asked about their attitudes to the role the Assembly should play in any development of the current tri-partite structure.   But most people present indicated that they thought it would not be wise to give the Assembly any control over policing in this transitional phase. The Assembly itself is a fledgling institution which should be allowed to develop before further powers are given to it - especially in the area of policing.

In a general survey of key points, it was felt that standards needed to be set in the context of international human rights provisions, and that those bodies and groups established to monitor the application of those standards should be representative of society in terms of gender, class, politics etc. The new force cannot see itself as policing only one half of the community.   Nor can we allow that attempts to create a more pluralist and representative force create even greater hostility - for insights into this problem see the NI Affairs Committee report last year. A more representative force must be seen as something that is of benefit to police, as well as to the communities served, and this realisation should create the necessary political will and management commitment to bring about effective change. Abuses of the past, particularly those involving the use of lethal force, must be avoided by creating a more effective legal framework, by incorporating human rights training into such things as weapons training, and by making the inquest system (a key tool for effective accountability) more accessible to families and other interested parties.

Workshop H

If we are to develop effective accountability we need to tilt the balance of control towards civil society. This means in turn that the police cannot determine their own agenda but need to involve the community in the process of policing. Partnerships between police and the communities served need to be developed and these partnerships will only prove possible if trust is established.

One big problem in this equation is what constitutes the community? We are not necessarily talking about a homogenous group of people, but we are probably talking of a grouping of people and organisations who work at the local level and already do, or are willing in future to, cooperate together for the benefit of the locality. Whatever structures are created must therefore provide a local forum for debate and control; such fora must be accessible; and they must find mechanisms which ensure that they move beyond simple (and sometimes brutal) majoritarianism and see the protection of rights as central to the project.

If the community is to get effectively involved in the process of policing they need to be involved in police training; they must also themselves get some training in monitoring and evaluating the police, so that they can engage equally in the debate about performance. The evolution of agreed performance indicators would be a very important tool for all involved.

Whatever structures are agreed, there needs to be more than one channel of communication - both between the police and the community, and between the local level and the policy level. Accountability will only work if it is multi-faceted and one level of information, involvement and control is influenced by and, in its turn, influences others.

List of conference participants

Attwood, Alex (Social Democratic and Labour Party)

Barboriak, Eric (US Consulate General)
Barten, Colm, (Bloody Sunday Initiative)
Bauknecht, Heidi (Pat Finucane Centre)
Beirne, Maggie (CAJ)
Bell, Christine (QUB)
Bell, Eileen (Alliance Party)
Blom-Cooper QC, Sir Louis (Ind. Commissioner for the Holding Centres)
Boyle, Dr. Michael (Secretariat - Commission on Policing)
Brady, Miriam (Conference of Religious in Ireland)
Brough, Emily (CAJ)
Bryan, Dominic (Democratic Dialogue)
Bunting, Mary (Fair Employment Commission)
Burns, Elaine (Ardoyne Association/Ardoyne Women' Forum)

Caleyron, Nathalie (CAJ)
Campbell, Joe (Mediation Network)
Campbell, Bea (SPEAKER)
Carlson, Dr. Helena (Democratic Left)
Cassidy, Fiona (Jones & Cassidy Solicitors)
Cavanaugh, Dr. Kathleen (Amnesty International)
Chapman, Alice (Community Safety Centre)
Chapman, Tim
Collins, Evelyn (Equal Opportunities Commission)
Cook, Barbary (Queerspace)
Crawshaw, Ralph (SPEAKER)
Cunneen, Mary , (Liberty)

Daniell, Jim (Criminal Justice Review)
de Brun, Bairbre (Sinn Fein)
Deighton, Jane (Human Rights Committee of the Law Society,
          England & Wales)
Delargy, Sr. Mary (Conference of Religious in Ireland)
Dillen, Nicole (Pat Finucane Centre)

Donoghue, David (Anglo Irish Secretariat)
Drummond, Bill (Greater Shankill Alternatives)

Edwards, Conor (CAJ)

Farrell, Michael (Irish Council for Civil Liberties)
Farrell, Niall (Relatives for Justice)
Fearon, Kate (NI Women's Coalition)
Feenan, Kathleen (Women's Information Group)
Finucane, Michael (Irish Council for Civil Liberties)
Finucane, Martin (Pat Finucane Centre)
Fitzpatrick, Prof. Barry (UU)
Fleming, Roy (RUC)
Foley, Nadette (Multi-Cultural Resource Centre)

Gadd, Briedge (Probation Board for Northern Ireland)
Gillen, Tom (Northern Ireland Committee-Irish Congress of Trade Unions)
Gilmore, Aideen (CAJ)
Gilleece, Br. Michael (Clonard Monastery)
Glackin, Jim (Commission for Racial Equality)
Gowan, Halya (Amnesty International)
Graham, Jane (Independent Commission for Police Complaints)
Greer, Chris (QUB)
Guillen, Francesc (SPEAKER)

Hall, Julia (Human Rights Watch)
Hainsworth, Colette (Relatives for Justice)
Halliday, Colin (Old Warren Partnership)
Hamilton, Michael
Haughey, Eilis
Hayes, Dr. Maurice (Commission on Policing for NI)
Hegarty, Angela (CAJ)
Heron, Stephen (Independent Commission for Police Complaints)
Holland, Mary (SPEAKER)
Holtzman, Zelda (SPEAKER)
Holywood, Brian (Rainbow Project)
Huens, Caroline (Belgian Gendarmerie)

Ilomeri, Pia

Jackson, Prof. John (Criminal Justice Review)
Jacobs, Pierre (Belgian Gendarmerie)
James, Mel (Law Society of England & Wales)
Jarman, Neil
Jasper, Lee (SPEAKER)
Johnston, Sam (Greater Shankill Alternatives)

Kane, Marian (Ardoyne Association/Ardoyne Women's Forum)
Kelly, Paddy (Children's Law Centre)
King, Stephen (Ulster Unionist Party)

Laird, Roly (RUC)
Lowry, John (Workers Party)

Madden, Peter (CAJ)
Mageean, Paul (CAJ)
Mann-Kler, Deepa (NICEM)
Maguire, Maryanne (International Federation of Radio Journalists)
Martin, Liz (CAJ)
Maye, Ian (Criminal Justice Review)
McCabe, Barbara (Ulster People's College)
McCabe, Eilis (Relatives for Justice)
McCabe, Jim (United Campaign Against Plastic Bullets)
McCann, May (Women into Politics)
McClean, Paddy Joe (Democratic Left)
McComb, Kenny (Lisburn Prisoners Support Project)
McCormick, Stephanie (Opportunity Youth)
McCotter, Rois (N. I Association for the Care and Resettlement of Offenders)
McCorry, Michael (Workers Party)
McDonald, Jim (Police Authority for Northern Ireland)
McDonough, Roisin (West Belfast Partnership)
McEvoy, Kieran (CAJ)
McGarry, Kevin (Relatives for Justice)
McGivern, John (Foundry Regeneration Trust)
McIlveen, Jim (Independent Commission for Police Complaints)
McKee, Eamonn (Department of Foreign Affairs)

McMahon, Mary (Democratic Left)
McNally, Geralyn (Bar Library)
McWilliams, Monica (NI Women's Coalition)
Mitchell, Jennifer (Independent Commission for Police Complaints)
Moore, Linda (CAJ)
Moran, Jade (QUB)
Mullan, Greg (Independent Commission for Police Complaints)
Mungoven, Rory (Amnesty International)
Murphy, Prof. Pauline (Training for Women Network)
Murphy, Donall (Murphy & Kerr Sols.)

Nelson, Rosemary (R. Nelson (sols))
Nelson, Ryan (Queerspace)
Nolan, Caroline (West Belfast Economic Forum)
Norris, Dr. Bill (Deputy Independent Commissioner for the Holding Centres)

O'Brien, Martin (CAJ)
O'Donnell, Val (Anglo-Irish Secretariat)
O'Doherty, Tony (Bloody Sunday Initiative)
O'Kelly, Brian (Brownlow Integrated College)
Olayisade, Femi (Multi Cultural Resource Centre)
O'Neill, Loreene (Columbanus Community of Reconciliation)
O'Rawe, Mary (CAJ)
Ostermeyer, Dr. Malcolm (Secretariat - Police Authority for NI)
Otty, Tim (Human Rights Committee of the Bar, England & Wales)
Otty, Maria

Park, Andrew (Community Dialogue)
Power, Danny (Frank Gillen Centre)
Price-Stephens, Richard

Quilley, Alan (Quaker House)
Quilley, Janet (Quaker House)
Quinn, Ciaran (Falls Community Council)

Randall, Laurel (Mediation Network)
Reynolds, Fr. Gerry (Clonard Monastery)
Rice, Geraldine (Police Authority for NI)

Robinson, Tessa (Lawyers Committee for Human Rights)
Rogers, Simon (Northern Ireland Office)
Russell, Supt. Keith (RUC)

Scraton, Phil (SPEAKER)
Smith QC, Peter (Commission on Policing for NI)
Solley QC, Stephen (Human Rights Committee of the Bar, England & Wales)
Sterling, David (Secretariat - Police Authority for NI)
Stone, Francis (Falls Community Council)

Tennant, Alexandra (Mediation Network)
Thompson, Alwyn (Evangelical Contribution on Northern Ireland)
Thompson, Ruth (Secretariat - Police Authority for NI)
Thompson, Mark (Relatives for Justice)
Tipping, Alan (Secretariat - Commission on Policing)

Ward, Heather (SPEAKER)
Waters, Debbie (Greater Shankill Alternatives)
Weir, Catherine
White, Mr. Brian (Criminal Justice Review)
Wilkinson, Oliver (Victim Support NI)
Williams, Sue
Winter, Jane (British Irish Rights Watch)

Yu, Patrick (NI Council for Ethnic Minorities)

CHAPTER TWO

Human Rights Benchmarks for policing change

Human Rights Benchmarks
for policing change

T he headings below follow the terms of reference set for the Policing Commission in the Good Friday Agreement. Under each rubric, information is given initially about the findings of the policing conference organised in Belfast by the CAJ on 26-27 February 1999 (see Chapter One for full details of the conference) followed by specific recommendations (or human rights benchmarks). The recommendations relate to:

- Composition, recruitment and training
- Culture, ethos and symbols
- Structures and management
- Accountability
- Transition and Management of Change

Composition, Recruitment and Training

a. *Findings of the policing conference*

A number of issues around composition, recruitment and training were debated at the CAJ conference. There was little dispute that current arrangements are unacceptable and at no point was "no change" in this regard proffered as a viable option. Disagreement lay more in the extent of transformation required, and how such transformation might best be brought about. The following points were communicated with particular resonance.

- With regard to composition and recruitment, outreach measures, affirmative action, and specific recruitment criteria, could prove effective in redressing the current imbalances. The concept of 'merit', for example, is of vital importance, but 'merit' (like beauty) can be in the eye of the beholder: the concept must be defined clearly and be rigorously assessed. The conference discussed, alongside issues of outreach, the fact that there will be a need for fewer police, and accordingly a reduction in numbers. Consideration will have to be given to lay-offs, and a series of legal reforms etc., within the context of a fair and open system that avoids random scape-goating of individual officers.

- It is essential to develop and sustain a human rights culture within police organisations. Consideration of international examples of policing change could prove instructive in this regard. The Catalonian experience, in particular, emphasised the value of pre-recruitment strategies geared at securing suitable applicants.

- The protection of human rights might in practice prove to be a unifying theme since, if it were taken as a guiding principle, it should ensure that the police did all the other things expected of them (upholding the law, serving the community, and so on).

- Policing does not happen within a political vacuum. Discourses on composition, recruitment and training must avoid seeking solutions that isolate individuals and their behaviour. It is critical that the police are recognised as an institution operating within a political context, and exercising extensive powers. To cite one of the conference working party reports: *"Emergency powers undermine good policing, and there is little point in talking of community relations, training, mechanisms for accountability, changing the composition of the force, as long as such powers are retained".*

- To facilitate what must constitute fundamental changes to current policing arrangements, measures to civilianise the police service will be critical.

- To ensure that what police officers learn 'in theory' is applied effectively and consistently 'in practice', basic human rights training and education should be continually revisited, in line with principles around 'life long learning'.

- Training might usefully include attendance at community colleges, both to educate police officers about human rights and the need for cultural awareness, and to educate communities about how to interact effectively and develop relationships of trust.

- Those involved in the process of training officers must of course represent the diversity of the community to be served.

b.   Human Rights Benchmarks

In light of these findings, and the submissions of different international and local human rights groups, the Commission on Policing should recommend:

1. Specific, ambitious, but realistic, targets and timetables for change in composition.   Achieving these targets will require that specific pro-active measures are taken to increase representation, at all levels of the police service, of Catholics, nationalists, women, ethnic minorities etc.(for detailed examples see note 1 at end of chapter). Alongside such changes - and not as an alternative to them - independent research should be commissioned into the current barriers to recruitment. Resources must be set aside to ensure that recommendations arising from such research can be put into practice.

2. Whatever future staffing options are decided upon, the Commission should recommend the need for clear recruitment criteria for appointing officers. Apart from needing such criteria to make decisions in the short term about current staff and the appropriateness or otherwise of retaining or re-hiring them, such criteria will help over the longer term to define what constitutes 'merit'. Developing a police service with a truly representative workforce will require an adequate definition of 'merit', but once clearly defined, 'merit' should obviously be the crucial guiding principle in any appointment process (see note 2 at end of chapter). Such criteria will also in future help in the process of weeding out under-performing officers and so-called 'bad apples' - see note 3 at end of chapter).

3. There should be a clear mission statement introduced covering new policing arrangements together with a new oath. Both of these will highlight the loyalty of individual officers and the institution as a whole to the rule of law and to human rights.

4. Concrete proposals for much greater civilian involvement at every stage in police training - design, delivery, and evaluation - are needed. Examples

of the kinds of measures which might be proposed by the Commission are attached in note 4 at the end of this chapter).

5. The proposals to changes in training must reflect the need for constant adaptation and flexibility in policing response. Moreover, the Commission's training recommendations must include the needs for regular in-service training, rather than focus solely on new recruits or on the managerial ranks.

6. Proposed changes to the training curriculum must indicate how basic principles of human rights, cultural awareness, impartiality, and accountability, will infuse all aspects of police work, and will be translated into practical effect "on the street". Human rights groups would want to see evidence that the Policing Commission has recommended the full and effective integration of human rights standards right across the training curriculum of all officers. They would also want to be assured that serious consideration had been given to relating formal training modules to the practical demands made of police officers, since anything less will prove irrelevant and be quickly set aside.

7. Training programmes in future will need to reflect the aspiration of a less militaristic, macho, uni-dimensional force, and therefore will need to put greater emphasis on skills such as team building, problem-solving, conflict resolution etc.

Culture, Ethos and Symbols

a.   *Findings of the policing conference*

There was some feeling among conference participants that it could prove useful to introduce a register of outside interests for police officers, in which membership of organisations such as the Orange Order or the Ancient Order of Hibernians would be declared. It has also been argued that such membership be completely prohibited. Yet, in either scenario, there is the issue of the officers' rights to privacy. No agreement proved possible but the following points received significant levels of support from the participants.

- The current symbols of the police force alienate certain members of the community.

- Symbols often give external voice to an internal culture. If police officers are to be successfully recruited from the whole community, and just as importantly retained, the organisational culture of policing, as well as its symbols, has to reflect diversity.

- In light of this, the adoption of neutral symbols and the recognition of different languages and cultures, in parallel with the transformation of current recruitment and training procedures, could contribute to the creation of a 'neutral working environment' where all groups will feel at ease.

- Any measures implemented to effect significant change within the current police culture, for example steps to de-militarise or civilianise the service, must penetrate through to all areas of policing.

- Tokenistic measures will signally fail to produce satisfactory results.

b. *Human Rights Benchmarks*

Human rights groups will be testing the recommendations of the Commission on Policing against the need to create:

1. a neutral working environment. Since all public bodies in Northern Ireland are expected to provide a neutral working environment for both their staff and the clientele served, the police should of course be no exception. Moreover, with the passage of the Northern Ireland Act 1998, all public bodies have a statutory duty to promote equality of opportunity. The police are not automatically covered by this legislative provision, but the Secretary of State can provide for this.[21] If such a designation has not

---

[21] The Northern Ireland Act 1998 in article 75 cites the various public authorities covered by the statutory duty to promote equality of opportunity and includes "any other person designated for the purposes of this section by order made by the Secretary of State". The RUC is not exempt from article 76 of the Act that renders religious and political discrimination unlawful.

occurred by the time the Policing Commission reports, this should be one of its recommendations.

2. a more civilian friendly culture (marching, saluting, passing out parades, ranks etc. should all be reviewed). Very important here is the extent of civilianisation across the service so that functions like recruitment, training, and indeed basic administrative tasks, be increasingly placed in the hands of people recruited from outside traditional policing circles. Moreover, it is fervently hoped that speedy steps can be taken to de-militarise policing, with a reduced use of fortified barracks, vehicles and heavily armoured equipment. The process of civilianisation should infuse policing itself and also ensure effective and constructive partnerships alongside internal changes.

3. a pluralist environment. It will be particularly important to ascertain that sectarian, sexist, racist, homophobic or other anti-rights dispositions are recognised and actively addressed at an early stage in the recruitment and training process. Indeed, testing and probationary periods could facilitate this process. However, as conference participants noted, it is difficult to know whether "isms" can be "trained out" of any institution. Anti-rights dispositions must therefore also be made amenable to clear disciplinary measures. Such practices, taken together with determined efforts to deal energetically with "hate crimes" of all descriptions, would assist in making the service responsive to the interests of under-represented groups.

In due course, in the words of one of the conference working parties: "If the police is to be 'ours' then it needs to be one where the symbols and culture reflect the diversity that is society".

Human rights principles (and therefore human rights groups) have no fixed notions of what constitutes a "neutral working environment", nor "civilianisation", nor indeed "pluralism". Nevertheless, it is clear that the proposals under the rubric of "culture, ethos and symbols" will be a key test for the Commission's recommendations and, if under-represented groups are to come forward in sufficient numbers, there must be a clear break with the legacy of the past.

Structures and Management

a.   *Findings of the policing conference*

The determination of specific models for the structure and management of policing in Northern Ireland is a lengthy and technical process. Differing levels of expertise among conference delegates, as well as obvious time constraints, impeded the translation of any shared views regarding inadequacies in the current system into formalised models for change. Despite these restrictions, however, there was a distinct sense of unanimity regarding what were considered certain key issues in the debate.

- An emphasis on human rights training and education must be a central feature of any new policing arrangements.

- The civilianisation of policing is of fundamental importance to establishing a police service which will both command support from and be accountable to the community as a whole.

- The design, implementation and maintenance of structural and managerial models should therefore involve an aggregation of bodies, both civilian and governmental, which coalesce around basic international human rights principles.

b.   *Human Rights Benchmarks*

Clearly policing structures differ from country to country and, from a human rights perspective, there is no single ideal structural model. Any study of international human rights principles does however help highlight the principles that need to infuse debates on policing structures.

Any structural model proposed by the Policing Commission will therefore need to aim at putting respect for human rights at the heart of the policing process by -
- Providing accountability - both legal and democratic (see on for more detailed discussion of this principle);

- Providing a police service which is civilian rather than military in philosophy, training and practice;
- Ensuring that any different forces which are created (eg along regional or functional lines) co-operate effectively;
- Securing a diverse and representative composition. People from both major traditions (and indeed all traditions) in Northern Ireland must be able to participate both in policing institutions and, just as importantly, in the structures of accountability. The creation of insular police forces at local level would contradict this goal of broad representativity;
- Providing an effective, responsive and efficient police service, adapted to the needs of the community served;
- Undermining rather than reinforcing the institutionalisation of existing social divisions and residential segregation patterns;
- Implementing a legal system which is itself framed according to international human rights standards;
- Avoiding either excessive centralisation and hierarchisation of authority, or a splintering and fragmenting that can lend itself to narrow "cronyism" or corruption;
- Effectively harnessing the commitment of local people to providing safe, crime-free environments;
- Keeping decision-making as close as possible to those being policed.

Accountability

a.   *Findings of the policing conference*

The issue of accountability, perhaps more than any other discussed at the conference, was a difficult area in which to make significant progress. It was particularly encouraging, then, that consensus was forthcoming on a number of important matters. The points receiving conspicuous support were as follows:

- Accountability arrangements will have to work at a variety of different levels - , whether it be at the level of new recruits or of senior management. Furthermore, accountability cannot be the responsibility of a single body; policing must be overseen by both internal and external regulatory mechanisms (see diagrams given in the presentation by Heather Ward pages 29 & 30). The task of holding the police to account should, therefore, be a shared undertaking, monitored by independent judicial and civic bodies to ensure that procedures are regulated in accordance with international human rights standards.

- Accountability to the community served will be of fundamental importance to any new policing arrangements. Serious consideration must therefore be given to the notion of what constitutes "community" (since there are geographic and non-geographic communities, for example, ethnic minorities). Measures must be implemented to ensure that community accountability is informed by, and respectful of, human rights. In addition, mechanisms for creating effective partnerships need to be established, along with clear guidelines as to the accountability of the community bodies that are established to oversee policing.

- Although there is no ideal model which can be simply imported from abroad, the consideration of international perspectives could be instructive in dealing with the current problems in Northern Ireland.

- The current complaints system must be seriously overhauled.

- The inquest system, which should be a crucial mechanism for effective police accountability, is currently inadequate. One important feature of an overhaul of current inquest procedures would be to make the system more accessible to families and interested parties. Furthermore, the development of a more effective legal framework in accordance with international human rights standards and principles will be central to real and effective change.

b. Human Rights Benchmarks

Accountability in policing has been a concern of human rights groups (international and domestic) over many years. CAJ wrote its first publication on this topic over ten years ago, in 1988. Despite references in some written submissions to the Policing Commission, and in public meetings, emphasising the wealth of accountability mechanisms in existence, it is the firm belief of independent observers that the legal framework has allowed and indeed facilitated a culture of impunity with regard to human rights abuses.

It is vital that the Policing Commission recommend a number of measures be taken with a view to ending this situation. As a minimum:

1. Emergency law must go. Abusive police powers will prevail if this basic step is not taken and other changes (whether in uniform, training, structures, or whatever) may well prove irrelevant.

2. Operational independence must be defined in law both positively, in terms of the kinds of decisions the Chief Constable can take, and negatively in terms of the powers held by other bodies (the Secretary of State, any successor body to the Police Authority etc.)

3. A whole series of institutional mechanisms need to be established to ensure that the Chief Constable and his/her officers are held fully to account. The current mechanisms of the Police Authority and the Community Police Liaison Committees have proved far from satisfactory, and various proposals have been made to give such civic oversight bodies more authority. One possible model for securing democratic accountability at the very local level is outlined in note 5 at the end of the chapter.

4. The Policing Commission will need to reflect upon and make specific recommendations regarding the policing changes necessitated by the detailed human rights and equality provisions of the Good Friday Agreement. Examples of such provisions include - incorporation of the European Convention, drafting of a Bill of Rights for Northern Ireland, the equality duty on public bodies, and the creation of Human Rights and Equality Commissions. Policing Commission recommendations regarding recruitment, training and police powers should clearly reflect these new and important safeguards.

5. International legal human rights principles need to be explicitly referred to in relevant police legislation and amendments will have to be proposed accordingly. Moreover, such principles need to be made

an integral part of police training, incorporated into the oath made by all new recruits, endorsed as part of the new policing mission statement. Special provision needs to be made to encourage a loyalty to this international human rights code with, for example, protections for "whistleblowing".

6.   The complaints system is being overhauled but the changes do not go far enough. Firstly, the Commission must comment on the need for sufficient resourcing of the Police Ombudsman's office, since without sufficient resources its ability to be entirely independent (a crucial test for its credibility) will be effectively undermined. Secondly, the Ombudsman must also be given the authority to investigate patterns of abuse rather than be restricted to individual cases and allegations of misbehaviour on the part of individual officers. Thirdly, and very importantly, the legal test for police complaints should be "the balance of probabilities" rather than "beyond a reasonable doubt" which is the current standard. Given that any move to discipline an officer currently requires the same standard of proof as if one were pursuing a criminal charge, it is hardly surprising that disciplinary measures are rarely taken.

7.   The audio and video recording of interviews with suspects ensures a minimal safeguard both in terms of detained suspects and in terms of vexatious complaints. The delays in introducing the necessary equipment were incomprehensible, and the Policing Commission should be able in its final report to confirm that the appropriate equipment is in place and in use. The necessary move away from emergency powers will allow the Commission to emphasise the importance of safeguards contained within legislation such as the Police and Criminal Evidence Act - most importantly, the necessity of having solicitors present during the interrogation of suspects.

8.   These safeguards should also reduce the possibility of threats being made against defence lawyers. The Policing Commission should take the opportunity of its report to emphasise the central importance of lawyers to the maintenance of the rule of law, and the need for government to ensure the safety of lawyers at all times.

9.   There is a clear need for a major overhaul of the inquest system. Currently there are even fewer legal protections for people in Northern Ireland killed in suspicious circumstances than in Britain, and in neither jurisdiction are the basic international standards being met. The most serious act a state can engage in is the killing of people within its jurisdiction: the legal framework providing scrutiny of such events must be above reproach, and it is clearly not. A detailed list of the kinds of changes that have been urged at different times by various human rights groups are included in note 6 at the end of this chapter.

10.   Most particularly, the standard for resort to the use of lethal force should be raised, in line with international human rights provisions. The provision for the use of lethal force in the Criminal Law Act (NI) 1967 is in line with general UK law which allows for such force "as is reasonable in the circumstances". This should be rescinded, and replaced by the international standard whereby law enforcement officials may resort to force only "when absolutely necessary", and in proportion to the threat posed. Since plastic bullets are treated as firearms for the purposes of current police guidelines and police training, their use in principle and in practice should be re-assessed in the light of the international human rights principles that govern the use of lethal force. The Policing Commission's attention is drawn to the fact that the UN Committee Against Torture recommended "the abolition of the use of plastic bullet rounds as a means of riot control" in November 1998.

11.   The use of informers should be better regulated to ensure effective oversight of this particularly sensitive area of police work. [22]

---

[22] A very extensive study of this issue was carried out in England by the organisation Justice. While the issues are not exactly the same in Northern Ireland, the fact that the system of using police informers both requires regulation, and is amenable to regulation, is well made in the study - "Under surveillance: Covert Policing and Human Rights Standards", July 1998.

Transition/ Management of Change

This rubric was not discussed in working parties at the conference, but was the focus of many of the plenary speeches (see in particular the contributions from Francesc Guillen and Zelda Holtzman, who spoke to changes introduced in Catalonia and South Africa respectively). Nevertheless, the debate around recruitment and accountability clearly raised questions about transition. In summary, several elements will be necessary to secure change on the ground.

Firstly there must be sufficient political will engendered behind the very concept and value of change as well as the specific changes proposed. It is vital that the Policing Commission seek to secure widespread political and public support for the need for change, and for its eventual recommendations. No-one under-estimates the difficulty of securing consensus around a topic as controversial as policing. At the same time, it will be difficult for bodies other than the Policing Commission to perform this vital function of developing support for a holistic programme of change that will bring about the new policing arrangements required. The changes proposed must be well-argued and offer neither cosmetic change, nor "change for change's sake". Instead the changes must be seen to offer a realistic hope of transforming a situation of abnormal policing (evolved over decades of division and serious conflict), into one in which a police service is able to operate effectively in a future that everyone hopes will be peaceful. The agenda of action outlined in this report is specifically intended to provide a constructive contribution to this effort.

Secondly, it is difficult for any society to move towards positive future change without any shared understanding of the legacy of the past. It is difficult if not impossible to see how the Policing Commission could secure such a shared understanding in the short time available to it and given its already huge brief. Nevertheless, its round of public meetings highlighted very powerfully the value of personal testimony and the need on the part of many for their pain to be heard. Whether one is the widow of someone shot by the police, or of a police officer who has been shot, one's pain deserves to be listened to with respect. Indeed, a close study of these different testimonies, starts an important process of understanding. The Commission's report should courageously address the differential experiences of policing. In any society, policing is experienced differently by the rich and the poor, by the young and the old, by men and women, by gays and straights, by blacks and whites etc.

How much truer is this likely to be in a society with deep communal divisions, heavily residentially segregated, and having experienced very high levels of violence, some directed specifically at the police? If we are to develop a police service that everyone can feel is "ours", and which represents a shared vision of what policing should be, then the Policing Commission can greatly assist in this interpretative process. The Commission should recount some of these differential experiences to ensure a greater understanding of the problems across the social, age, and political divisions of society; they should acknowledge the problems of the past; and they should seek to provide an objective starting point from which future policing arrangements can be discussed knowledgeably and sensitively.

Most importantly, the Policing Commission must test all its eventual recommendations and proposals against past experiences of policing. Theoretically, various checks and balances existed in the past to protect society against human rights abuses - yet report after report by various UN bodies and reputable international human rights groups highlighted that these checks and balances were not working. Why did allegations of collusion persist and which changes being proposed by the Policing Commission will ensure that this will become a problem of the past? What did the Stalker, Sampson and Stevens reports reveal of problems in the past, and why should we believe that future allegations of a shoot-to-kill policy will not arise, or if they do, that they can be effectively and rapidly investigated? How can we be sure in future that the past litany of unpublished inquiry reports will not continue? Why did reports of the intimidation of lawyers go unheeded, and result in a climate of hostility leading ultimately to the death of Rosemary Nelson? The Policing Commission will need to convince the readers of its report that, if their recommendations are put into practice, such tragedies will never happen again.

These questions are not in any sense intended to be rhetorical. If the changes proposed do not offer hope for real change on the ground, the Policing Commission's recommendations will not secure the necessary support and will certainly fail. Every recommendation of the Policing Commission is likely to be tested against the problems of the past. They will certainly be tested against the hope they offer for change in the future.

Notes to Chapter Two

1.   Practical suggestions for pro-active recruitment measures

A large number of recruitment and promotion strategies are being used effectively by police in other parts of the world to ensure a representative service, and some or all of these might prove useful in Northern Ireland, e.g.

- Legislative changes to allow affirmative action.
- Outreach measures (advertising, leafleting, targeted translations and distribution of promotional materials);
- Bridging schemes;
- Target setting and the monitoring of the targets;
- Lateral entry schemes;
- Mentoring schemes;
- Fast-tracking;
- Regular reviews of selection processes inc. review of person and job specifications;
- Regular reviews of testing processes inc. pre-recruitment strategies;
- Tie break schemes

2.   Definitions of merit

In a study of the concept of merit for the Employment Equality Review, Dr Chris McCrudden cited four radically different conceptions of merit[23]. The first is where the term is used as a synonym for the absence of direct discrimination, cronyism or political favouritism. In this sense, the merit principle is fulfilled if the process by which job allocation decisions are reached is not tainted by these factors. The second conception of merit is where there is a general relatedness between means and ends. Merit, in this conception, would amount to the "possession of qualities that are thought to be of general value in the society and are reasonably likely to prove useful in carrying out a

---

[23] Material taken from "The Merit Principle and Fair Employment in Northern Ireland" by Chris McCrudden, SACHR Employment Equality in NI, volume I, 1996; see also Oxford Journal of Legal Studies, volume 18, 1998.

specific function". This conception would allow one, for example, to use 'A level grades' in history and English literature in hiring trainee bank managers. Yet a third conception of merit is that of "strict job relatedness". This requires a much tighter fit between means and ends, and merit becomes the "possession of precisely those qualities of excellence needed to perform a functionally defined task".

The fourth conception of merit, and one that the CAJ has particularly commended to the Policing Commission for consideration is that which sees merit "as the capacity to produce results". This model tends to take a much broader view of what 'the job' amounts to, and is much more sympathetic to a view which includes, within the idea of the job, those features which assist in carrying it out rather than just those which are necessary in order to carry it out.

'Merit' is not an uncontested principle and it must therefore be made the subject of public debate and scrutiny, and be clearly defined. Only then will we be sure that future policing arrangements will facilitate rather than impede the creation of a more representative police service.

3. Possible criteria for appointing officers in the new policing arrangements

Human Rights Watch in a briefing paper for the Policing Commission argued that "Whether the force is reformed internally and affirmative steps are taken to attract Catholics, women and other minorities to the policing service, or the force is completely demobilised and starts from the bottom up with an entirely new pool of applicants, an *independent* vetting process that evaluates each and every RUC officer who served in the past and each new recruit will be essential". They suggest the following:

- The establishment of an effective and credible vetting unit;
- Vetting should be made a requirement for being a police officer;
- Procedural safeguards should be such as to protect the due process rights of all officers, including rights of appeal etc.
- An open process by which the vetting process is explained in detail to the public and methods for public participation are developed and advertised.

Human Rights Watch goes on to list the sources of information which amongst others should be considered confidentially in the course of the vetting process, and suggest:

- Certain classified government documents (eg Stalker/Sampson reports)
- Civil actions - court rulings and out-of-court settlements wherein officers have been involved in cases of assault, wrongful arrest, etc.
- Evidence of illegally obtained confessions (available in court documentation)
- Inquest depositions
- Official complaints
- Investigative files of the Director for Public Prosecutions
- Personnel files
- Community consultation - adverts; interviews with academics, journalists and others who might have information relating to individual officers;
- Input from expert domestic and international NGOs.

4. Measures to civilianise the training process

International experience suggests that the design and the delivery of training to police recruits should involve people other than just police officers. This can be done in a variety of ways:

- Involvement of civilian trainers in a police institute
- A civilian training institute administered by non-police personnel
- Training outside of any formal institute eg placement in a community group
- Accredited courses run in universities and colleges
- Mixture of formal police training intermingled with community service and/or work experience
- Practical courses offered by specialist groups outside of police ranks
- Training being offered by a variety of people, so that the diversity of the community to be served is modelled in the very training process - eg male and female trainers, representatives from ethnic minorities etc.

- Civilians to be involved in the formulation of the training programme, in the setting of its objectives, in its delivery, in its evaluation, and/or in its location.
- Development of active training partnerships with local groups - voluntary organisations, business, statutory agencies, local elected politicians, young people, and human rights activists.
- Include civilian input into special research or policy arms within police structures.

5.   One possible model for securing democratic accountability

It was previously suggested that the model of District Partnerships might be a useful one to emulate when creating localised civic oversight bodies for policing. These Partnerships were specially created as a delivery mechanism for some of the European Peace and Reconciliation funds, and have by-and-large been hailed as one of the success-stories of the programme overall. Some of the characteristics that make these Partnerships successful can be summed up as follows:

- **Locally-based:** The members are people who live and/or work in the area and therefore possess expert local knowledge.

- **Cross-sectoral:** Consisting as they do of one-third local Councillors, one-third community and voluntary sector representatives, and one-third business/trade union and statutory representatives, the Partnerships are multi-sectoral. This composition brings together a mix of elected and appointed people; business and trade unionists; people representing political parties and communities of very different political perspectives, etc. Every attempt is made to ensure a mix of people by gender, age etc.

- **Clear remit:** The Partnerships have a specific remit that they are expected to carry out and clear guidelines about this remit.

- **Operating guidelines:** In particular, the Partnerships have clear operating guidelines. They must work in a transparent way; they must be accountable to the local community and to the NI Partnership Board; they must develop a clear strategic vision for the locality, in conjunction with and in response to bottom-up involvement by local people; they must agree at all times to determine and then work within fair decision making procedures; they must develop a participative, empowering approach and not become local "gate-keepers" etc.

- **Budgetary authority**: They have a clear budget to work within and dispense as they think best, though clearly this is to be done within the remit and operating guidelines established for them at the NI-wide level.

6.   Changes required to the inquest system

The following recommendations have been made to the UK authorities on numerous occasions regarding the holding of inquests

- An inquest should always be held into a disputed death.
- Coroners should always sit with a jury in disputed cases.
- Inquests should be held promptly and adjournments kept to a minimum.
- Legal aid should be made available for inquests.
- The notion of parties to an inquest should be introduced, and parties should have the right to examine witnesses and challenge jurors.
- Material witnesses should be entitled to testify.
- Coroners should have the power to compel material witnesses to attend and testify, subject to their being protected from self-incrimination.
- Hearsay evidence should not be admissible.
- Juries should be entitled to bring in appropriate recommendations for the avoidance of further deaths.
- Coroners and juries should be entitled to deliver their verdicts.

CAJ has previously proposed the establishment of a committee to review the functioning of inquests in Northern Ireland. The committee should include coroners, lawyers with experience of inquests, representatives of the Northern Ireland Office and Lord Chancellor's Department, the NI Human Rights Commission, and relevant civil liberties and human rights organisations. Its terms of reference should include:

- Drawing up criteria for a fair and effective system of inquests into disputed deaths which conforms with internationally-accepted standards.
- Re-defining the remit of inquests to encompass those criteria.
- Recommending amendments to the legislation governing inquests in order to give effect to those criteria.

Appendices

Appendix 1

Extracts from Good Friday Agreement

POLICING AND JUSTICE

1.   The participants recognise that policing is a central issue in any society. They equally recognise that Northern Ireland's history of deep divisions has made it highly emotive, with great hurt suffered and sacrifices made by many individuals and their families, including those in the RUC and other public servants. They believe that the agreement provides the opportunity for a new beginning to policing in Northern Ireland with a police service capable of attracting and sustaining support from the community as a whole. They also believe that this agreement offers a unique opportunity to bring about a new political dispensation which will recognise the full and equal legitimacy and worth of the identities, senses of allegiance and ethos of all sections of the community in Northern Ireland. They consider that this opportunity should inform and underpin the development of a police service representative in terms of the make-up of the community as a whole and which, in a peaceful environment, should be routinely unarmed.

2.   The participants believe it essential that policing structures and arrangements are such that the police service is professional, effective and efficient, fair and impartial, free from partisan political control; accountable, both under the law for its actions and to the community it serves; representative of the society it polices, and operates within a coherent and co-operative criminal justice system, which conforms with human rights norms. The participants also believe that those structures and arrangements must be capable of maintaining law and order including responding effectively to crime and to any terrorist threat and to public order problems. A police service which cannot do so will fail to win public confidence and acceptance. They believe that any such structures and arrangements should be capable of delivering a policing service, in constructive and inclusive partnerships with the community at all levels, and with the maximum delegation of authority and responsibility, consistent with the foregoing principles. These arrangements should be based

on principles of protection of human rights and professional integrity and should be unambiguously accepted and actively supported by the entire community.

3.   An independent Commission will be established to make recommendations for future policing arrangements in Northern Ireland including means of encouraging widespread community support for these arrangements within the agreed framework of principles reflected in the paragraphs above and in accordance with the terms of reference at Annex A. The Commission will be broadly representative with expert and international representation among its membership and will be asked to consult widely and to report no later than Summer 1999.

4.   The participants believe that the aims of the criminal justice system are to:
- deliver a fair and impartial system of justice to the community;
- be responsive to the community's concerns, and encouraging community involvement where appropriate;
- have the confidence of all parts of the community; and
- deliver justice efficiently and effectively.

5.   There will be a parallel wide-ranging review of criminal justice (other than policing and those aspects of the system relating to the emergency legislation) to be carried out by the British Government through a mechanism with an independent element, in consultation with the political parties and others. The review will commence as soon as possible, will include wide consultation, and a report will be made to the Secretary of State no later than Autumn 1999.

6.   Implementation of the recommendations arising from both reviews will be discussed with the political parties and with the Irish Government.

7.   The participants also note that the British Government remains ready in principle, with the broad support of the political parties, and after consultation, as appropriate, with the Irish Government, in the context of ongoing implementation of the relevant recommendations, to devolve responsibility for policing and justice issues.

(Extracts from Good Friday Agreement continued)

ANNEX A

COMMISSION ON POLICING FOR NORTHERN IRELAND

Terms of Reference

Taking account of the principles on policing as set out in the agreement, the Commission will inquire into policing in Northern Ireland and, on the basis of its findings, bring forward proposals for future policing structures and arrangements, including means of encouraging widespread community support for those arrangements.

Its proposals on policing should be designed to ensure that policing arrangements, including composition, recruitment, training, culture, ethos and symbols, are such that in a new approach Northern Ireland has a police service that can enjoy widespread support from, and is seen as an integral part of, the community as a whole.

Its proposals should include recommendations covering any issues such as re-training, job placement and educational and professional development required in the transition to policing in a peaceful society.

Its proposals should also be designed to ensure that:

- the police service is structured, managed and resourced so that it can be effective in discharging its full range of functions (including proposals on any necessary arrangements for the transition to policing in a normal peaceful society);
- the police service is delivered in constructive and inclusive partnerships with the community at all levels with the maximum delegation of authority and responsibility;
- the legislative and constitutional framework requires the impartial discharge of policing functions and conforms with internationally accepted norms in relation to policing standards;
- the police operate within a clear framework of accountability to the law and the community they serve, so:
  - they are constrained by, accountable to and act only within the law;

- their powers and procedures, like the law they enforce, are clearly established and publicly available;
- there are open, accessible and independent means of investigating and adjudicating upon complaints against the police;
- there are clearly established arrangements enabling local people, and their political representatives, to articulate their views and concerns about policing and to establish publicly policing priorities and influence policing policies, subject to safeguards to ensure police impartiality and freedom from partisan political control;
- there are arrangements for accountability and for the effective, efficient and economic use of resources in achieving policing objectives;
- there are means to ensure independent professional scrutiny and inspection of the police service to ensure that proper professional standards are maintained;
- the scope for structured co-operation with the Garda Siochana and other police forces is addressed; and
- the management of public order events which can impose exceptional demands on policing resources is also addressed.

The Commission should focus on policing issues, but if it identifies other aspects of the criminal justice system relevant to its work on policing, including the role of the police in prosecution, then it should draw the attention of the Government to those matters.

The Commission should consult widely, including with non-governmental expert organisations, and through such focus groups as they consider it appropriate to establish.

The Government proposes to establish the Commission as soon as possible, with the aim of it starting work as soon as possible and publishing its final report by Summer 1999.

Appendix 2

Short Bibliography

Many submissions to the Policing Commission were drawn upon by CAJ in drawing up the human rights benchmarks for policing change. Below are the submissions from international human rights organisations -

♦ Briefing paper for the Independent Commission on Policing for Northern Ireland - Recommendations for Vetting the Police Force in Northern Ireland, Human Rights Watch, 16 January 1999.

♦ United Kingdom - Submission by Amnesty International to the Independent Commission on Policing for Northern Ireland, November 1998

♦ Report by the Lawyers Committee for Human Rights on mission to Northern Ireland and submission to Policing Commission (forthcoming)

Appendix 3

Major CAJ Publications[24]

No. 1   **The Administration of Justice in Northern Ireland:** the proceedings of a conference held in Belfast on June 13th, 1981 (no longer in print)

No. 2   **Emergency Laws in Northern Ireland:** a conference report, 1982 (no longer in print)

No. 3   **Complaints Against the Police in Northern Ireland**, 1982. (price £2.50)

No. 4   **Procedures for Handling Complaints Against the Police**, 1983 (updated by pamphlet No.16)

No. 5   **Emergency Laws: suggestions for reform in Northern Ireland**, 1983 (price £1.50)

No. 6   **Consultation between the Police and the Public**, 1985 (price £3.00)

No. 7   **Ways of Protecting Minority Rights in Northern Ireland**, 1985 (price £4.00)

No. 8   **Plastic Bullets and the Law**, 1985 (updated by pamphlet No. 15) (see also Plastic Bullets briefing No. 40)

No. 9   **"The Blessings of Liberty":** An American Perspective on a Bill of Rights for Northern Ireland, 1986 (price £2.50)

No. 10 **The Stalker Affair: More questions than answers**, 1988 (price £3.00)

No. 11 **Police Accountability in Northern Ireland,** 1988 (price £2.00)

No. 12 **Life Sentence and SOSP Prisoners in Northern Ireland,** 1989 (price £1.50)

No. 13 **Debt - An Emergency Situation?** A history of the Payments for Debt Act in Northern Ireland and its effects on public employees and people on state benefits, 1989 (price £2.00)

No. 14 **Lay Visitors to Police Stations in Northern Ireland**, 1990 (price £2.00)

No. 15 **Plastic Bullets and the Law**, 1990 (price £2.00)

No. 16 **Cause for Complaint:** The system for dealing with complaints against the police in Northern Ireland, 1990 (price £2.00)

No. 17 **Making Rights Count.** Includes a proposed Bill of Rights for Northern Ireland, 1990 (price £3.00)

No. 18 **Inquests and Disputed Killings in Northern Ireland**, 1992 (price £3.50)

No. 19 **The Casement Trials:** A Case Study on the Right to a Fair Trial in Northern Ireland, 1992 (price £3.00)

---

[24] This list is an abbreviated version of the CAJ Publications Catalogue. For full details of all CAJ publications and submissions contact the CAJ office.

No. 20   **Racism in Northern Ireland:** The need for legislation to combat racial discrimination in Northern Ireland, the proceedings of a CAJ conference held on 30th November 1992, (price £3.00)

No. 21   **A Bill of Rights for Northern Ireland**, 1993 (price £2.00)

No. 22   **Staid agus Stadas Gaeilge i dTuaisceart na hEireann** - The Irish Language in Northern Ireland: The UK Government's approach to the Irish Language in light of the European Charter for Regional or Minority Languages, 1993 (price £3.50/IR£3.50)

No. 23   **A Fresh look at Complaints against the Police**, 1993 (price £3.50/IR£3.50)

No. 24   **Adding Insult to Injury?** Allegations of Harassment and the use of Lethal Force by the Security Forces in Northern Ireland, 1994 (price £3.50/IR£3.50)

No. 25   **The States We are In: Civil Rights in Ireland, North and South -** proceedings of a conference held in Dublin by the Irish Council of Civil Liberties and the CAJ, 1993 (price £3.50)

No. 26   **Civil Liberties in Northern Ireland: The CAJ Handbook** (2nd edition), June 1993 (price £6.00)

No. 27   **"Harassment: It's part of life here..."** Survey of young people's attitudes to and experience of harassment by the security forces, December 1994 (price £5.00)

No. 28   **No Emergency, No Emergency Law: Emergency Legislation related to Northern Ireland the case for repeal**, March 1995 (price £4.00)

No. 29   **Right to Silence debate**, the Northern Ireland Experience (May 1994) (price £3.00)

No. 30   **Human Rights: The Agenda for Change - Human Rights, the Northern Ireland Conflict and The Peace Process** (includes proceedings of a conference held in Belfast on 11ᵗʰ & 12ᵗʰ March 1995), December 1995 (price £3.50)

No. 31   **Fair Employment For All**: Submission to the Standing Advisory Commission on Human Rights on Fair Employment, February 1996 (price £4.00)

No. 32   **The Misrule of Law:** A report on the policing of events during the Summer of 1996 in Northern Ireland, October 1996 (price £5.00)

No. 33   **Mainstreaming Fairness?**: A discussion paper by Dr. Christopher McCrudden, on "Policy Appraisal and Fair Treatment", November 1996 (price £3.00)

No. 34   Mainstreaming Fairness, **"Policy appraisal and Fair Treatment"**, A summary of a consultation process around "Policy Appraisal & Fair Treatment", June 1997 (price £2.00)

No. 35   **Making a Bill of Rights Stick: Options for implementation in Northern Ireland**, A discussion paper, September 1997 (price £2.50)

No. 36   **Policing the Police : A Report on the Policing of Events During the Summer of 1997 in Northern Ireland,** November 1997 (Price £2.00)
No. 37   **Human Rights on Duty: Principles for better policing - International lessons for Northern Ireland.** December 1997 (Price £6.00)
No. 38   **Civil Liberties in Northern Ireland: The CAJ Handbook (3rd edition),** December 1997 (Price £7.00)
No. 39   **Benchmarks for Change: A Proposal by Dr. Christopher McCrudden on Mainstreaming Fairness in the Governance of Northern Ireland,** February 1998 (Price £2.00)
No. 40   **Plastic bullets briefing paper,** June1998 (Price £3.00)
No. 41   **A Guide to Prisoners' Rights and Prison Law in Northern Ireland,** September 1998 (Price £5.00)

Over eighty submissions to local, national and international bodies are also available. For a full Publications Catalogue and/or for details on membership, please contact:

**CAJ,
45/47 Donegall Street,
Belfast BT1 2FG**

Tel: (02890) 232394.